Digital Influencer

A Guide to Achieving Influencer Status Online

By John Lincoln

Table of Contents

Chapter 1: Developing an Influencer Mindset
Critical Components to Becoming a Real Influencer
Three Types of Influencers – Who Will You Be?
The Science and Psychology of Influence
How You Can Use Targeted Content to Grow Your Influence

Chapter 2: Becoming an Influencer
How to Gain Influence Through Blogging
Secrets to Guest Posting Like a Pro
How You Can Use SEO to Drive Your Authority
Be Innovative, Have Something to Say and Be Listened To
Why and How You Need to Educate Others
How to Befriend Influencers and Leverage Each Other
Social Media Sites You Should Be Looking At
Be Smart with Your Time, Select Sites that Matter

Chapter 3: Getting Advanced, Getting Innovative, Getting Seen
Smart Tools to Give You the Edge Most People Fail to Find
Why You Will Lose Without Social Media Ads and Where to Run
Them
Using the New Wave of Native Advertising to Get Content over Ten
Times the Reach
How You Can Use Viral Marketing Concepts for Exponential Reach

Chapter 4: Your Personal Plan of Action
The Most Important Part: Creating Your Influencer Plan of Action
Influencer Self Evaluation: Must Ask Questions
The Timeline: Review, Absorb, Customize, Become
Final Takeaways

Foreword

John Lincoln is Co-Founder and CEO of Ignite Visibility, an instructor at the University of California San Diego, an entrepreneur, an author and an award-winning industry expert.

With over 10 years of experience in this ever-evolving and demanding industry, John Lincoln has worked on well over 400 Internet marketing campaigns, including many global brands, Fortune 500 companies and products with common household names. Lincoln has generated millions of dollars in revenue for clients, authored thousands of blogs and articles, taken multiple websites to number one positions in Google for competitive keywords and built social communities by hundreds of thousands of members.

Lincoln has taught at the University of California San Diego since 2010 and currently teaches courses on search engine optimization, social media marketing, conversion rate optimization, online advertising and analytics. He is also a corporate trainer and writer for Search Engine Land, Marketing Land, Search Engine Journal, Entrepreneur Magazine and Inc. Magazine. Lincoln has been featured by Forbes, Good Morning San Diego, San Diego Union Tribune, CIO Magazine, Business Insider and many other media outlets. Lincoln has been named one of the most influential people in conversion rate optimization, earned the title of top SEO expert of the year and has won awards for his work in social media.

Lincoln holds an MBA in Finance from Alliant International University and a BA in Literature from the University of California Santa Cruz. He is certified in Google Analytics and Google AdWords. Outside of professional life, Lincoln is also an avid surfer and soccer player, as well as a father, husband and active member in the community.

Lincoln is an enthusiastic Internet marketing expert who studies around the clock. His business mission is to help others through Internet marketing and he takes great pride in his work. You can follow him on Twitter @johnelincoln

Digital Influencer

A Guide to Achieving Influencer Status Online

Definition Digital Influencer: An online persona with the power to stimulate the mindset and affect the decisions of others through real or perceived authority, knowledge, position, distribution or relationships.

I am not going to hold anything back in this book. But neither can you if you want to be an influencer. You have to fully dedicate yourself, otherwise it is impossible. Are you ready? Let's go!

It is possible that someday soon you will have an amazing service, product or idea that will change your industry forever. Perhaps you already have a start-up for that industry-changing service, product or idea and a crack team to make it work. Or maybe you are just entering into a traditional industry that is highly competitive. So now you just open up shop and have the business rolling in, right? No! Sorry, it is not that easy. Every business that dominates − I mean really dominates a market − needs someone with real influence running it. Without influence, your company will always be missing out on a key factor for success.

Too often, people believe that influencers are born, not made, and that we can't learn how to do what they do. Wrong!

Influencers do not pop up overnight; they work incredibly hard to get where they are. Just ask them. In most cases, someone in a specific industry has been working hard for 10, 20 even 30 years before they can be legitimately called - an influencer − and by that I mean a person who is really among the top 50 of the primary movers in an industry. But you can become an influencer much more quickly if you are focused and know the right steps to take.

This practical guide to becoming an influencer in your industry will explain what influence is and how it works. It will show you how to grow your following, build credibility and develop your identity as an authority in your field. It will provide direction in how to educate yourself, create compelling content, -harness the power of social media and engage with your community. It will teach you how to build an online persona that is so powerful, a simple social media update or blog post will be able to affect change in your industry.

This process works. I have done this for myself and hundreds of clients. This book is your shortcut to reaching influencer status fast. Instead of wasting decades or even your entire life trying to figure out what you need to do, I'm just going to tell you how it works. I'll also help you develop a personal plan.

That is my promise to you in this book. But in order for you to get the most out of this book I need something from you. While you read this book, I need you to take notes, complete the action items in each section and consider how each of these concepts, tools and strategies applies specifically to your goals. Can you promise me that? Okay then, let's keep going.

I am going to start off by giving you some important background information and concepts that are critical to know if you want to become an influencer. As we progress, I will give you more specifics regarding tools, strategies and even a timeline. But first things first: what are we talking about here?

Chapter 1: Developing an Influential Mindset

Before becoming an effective influencer you must have the right mindset. This chapter will provide you with strategies for achieving your goal, starting with the components necessary for becoming an online influencer, the types of influencers, a bit about the psychology of influence and explaining how you can use targeted content to increase your influence.

Critical Components to Becoming a Real Influencer

Influencer marketing is one of the most effective ways to target the consumers who want what you have to offer. Among all of the marketing noise on the Internet, influencers grab the attention of consumers and drown out the millions of other pieces of content online. If a normal person and an influencer publish the same piece of content, the influencer's content gets read and shared an exponential number of times, while the normal person's content barely gets noticed. Why is this?

The research shows that, as a rule, influencers do three main things:[1]

- Influencers have an effective "echo," meaning that they can mobilize opinions and create reactions.

- Influencers have powerful "exposition," which means that they have large communities and audiences focused on specific issues in which they have expertise.

- Influencers get a major "share of voice," in other words, they are participating with the most frequency and authority in conversations about their focus area and, as such, are the participants most revered in these conversations.

---

[1]Augure (2014). *The 2014 Influencer Marketing Status Report* (online version). http://www.augure.com/wp-content/uploads/2014/02/Influencers-marketing-Report-2014-Augure.pdf

Influencers use thought leadership, technology, talent and other tools to influence others to take action. Influencers are the people others come to for advice. They have a genuine, loyal following because they add real value to their industries. Influencers have insight and actionable information, and because of that they attract the eye of even major brands.

In short: influencers have power, and they use that power to catalyze actions in others. With this power comes the ability to drive a business straight to the top, knock down the competition, or alter the course of an entire industry in some cases. The level of impact, of course, all depends on how powerful the influencer actually is.

There is an endless stream of information out there, and everyone is looking for content that is actionable, credible and powerful. Most of us are on the seeking side of things—we consume the best information we can find.

But authorities create that high-quality

information. They consume, but they also create. As you produce more and more valuable content, you grow your influence. There are so many blogs online that say nothing! Real bloggers, real influencers, they say something you cannot get anywhere else. They go the extra mile, they give it all away, they put in the extra hours and then some, and it pays off.

Influencers spark conversations and keep them blazing. They nurture useful, productive relationships and networks, and they continue to improve themselves and their work. Becoming an influencer is an ongoing process. It does not ever stop. You must always be pushing your work to the next level, or you will lose that power of influence. You must constantly be evolving, growing and contributing.

This matters because it dictates the necessity of engaging at a high-level continually. As new consumers of your content find you, they will research you, what you do and who you know, as they watch your social media profiles and activities. They will want more and more. So, it is up to you to constantly be improving to remain an influencer in the eyes of your current following and to attract new followers.

One bad piece of content, unfortunately, can turn the tide and result in losing a percentage of that clout.

Three Types of Influencers – Which Will You Be?

Influencers are everywhere – in different forms, different circles and with varied levels of authority. As human beings, we all influence each other.

Micro Influencer – Someone who influences a small circle of people.

> **Example Micro Influencer:** Let's say you are about to become a parent for the first time, and you want to know which doctor and hospital to use for the birth. Do you read what doctors and hospitals say about themselves – copy that was

written for the web by someone else? You might, but chances are excellent that you value the opinions of people that you know and trust a lot more. You ask your social media friends and others you know who the best doctor is, and you take those recommendations seriously.

An influencer can be anyone, in any circle, on any level. It is anyone who is an authority and can inspire action in others. This is an example of a micro influencer, or someone who has influence but only for a small circle.

Subject Matter Expert Influencer - Someone who has significant influence over a specific subject and the industries that deal with that subject.

Example Subject Matter Expert Influencer: Let's say you are looking for a lawyer for your business. Would you be more likely to do research online or to reach out to the lawyer on social media who constantly publishes articles, acts as a guest speaker, makes videos and seems so passionate about what he or she does? This would be an influencer at the subject matter expert level.

A subject matter expert influencer attracts business through his or her influence, as well as impacts an industry.

Macro Influencer - Someone who has significant influence reaching a variety of subjects, industries and demographics.

Example Macro Influencer: When it comes to a macro influencer, take a moment to think about Oprah. When she recommends one book, it automatically becomes a best seller. Let that sink in. If you get her, or someone on a similar level (a macro influencer), to recommend your work, it is an automatic success. Now *that* is the power of influence on the highest level. Why do you think brands desperately try to align with celebrities? In some cases, brands will even launch a new product line, give a celebrity a percentage and ask them to promote it. It is a surefire formula for success.

But you don't need to be as influential or align with someone as powerful as Oprah. You just need the appropriate power of influence to help you reach the goals you have in your personal and professional life.

Whether your goals are large or small, it doesn't matter. It is what's important to you that matters. This means that the level or subject of influence you need to achieve for yourself should depend on what you want to achieve through that influence. That is a key point. It is important to know what you want out of life, personally, business-wise and spiritually. This basic self assessment is an essential first step. You need to know this, as well as define your goals, to determine the level of influencer and status you are looking to achieve.

In this book, we are talking about influencers

and business, and specifically, how you can be this kind of influencer for your company. Whether you are a company owner or a go-getter employee, you can do it. You can provide your company great value by becoming an influencer.

Influencers who are allies to your brand and do good work can cause a positive opinion about your company to spread. They send out actionable advice through their networks, and the ripples keep expanding outward. When you invite influencers into a conversation, they never come alone. They bring their network, and if the influencer is as powerful as Oprah, one million new people buy copies of your book. That is the truth. I have a client whose product was recommended by Oprah. It was life-changing.

Personally, I have seen the power of being an influencer, and I have learned and developed a process to become one. Over the last ten years, I have attacked this opportunity. I've blogged, taught, spoken at conferences, made videos, led webinars, participated on social media conversations and done almost anything else you can name in the Internet marketing space.

Ignite Visibility (the digital marketing agency I own with my talented and dedicated business partner Krish Coughran), now gets hundreds of leads each month through these channels and does millions of dollars in revenue a year. Every day, I have the absolutely genuine pleasure of meeting new people and re-connecting with important partners who enjoy working with someone like me (and our very talented team) – someone who is utterly passionate about what he does.

Now, let's talk about the science behind influence. To be an effective influencer, it is imperative to understand and practice these concepts.

The Science and Psychology of Influence

Influence over others isn't the result of luck, timing or sheer charisma. Influence is essentially applied science working in the marketplace. Certainly, some people may naturally find the science and psychology of influence intuitive, while for others, it takes more work. But this is always true in life.

Most of us weren't that person who aced every exam without cracking a book, and most of us will need to work to achieve influence. You must understand the science and psychology of influence to seize it. Fortunately, the research surrounding influence is clear and provides a detailed road-map for you to follow.

The Psychology of Influence

Robert Cialdini, a psychology and marketing professor and author, has named six principles of influence based on his experimental studies over the past 30 years.[2] To do this, he worked with people he titled "compliance professionals" – those who succeed in their work only when they successfully persuade others to take action.

---

[2] Cialdini, Robert, PhD. *Influence: The Psychology of Persuasion*, revised edition. New York: Harper Business Publishing, 2006.

For example, salespeople only succeed if they persuade you to buy.

Cialdini's work highlights the ways that each of us can interact with others more effectively to influence them. Interestingly, however, he has pointed out that you can only succeed as an influencer if you can persuade others that what you have to offer is unique and valuable.

This is a very important point. You cannot be an influencer unless you are doing something unique and valuable. You have to use this principal to guide all of your work. If you write a blog post that 4,000 others have written and you have not added anything new to the conversation, you have failed to further your path as an influencer.

Therefore, you must combine the technique and science of influence with genuinely beneficial content, ideas or services. Mastering these six concepts of the psychology of influence allows you to harness them for your own use as an influencer.

Reciprocity

The notion of treating others as you'd like to be treated doesn't belong to a particular group or faith; reciprocity is a basic truth of human nature. Help people. Help people. Help people.

It will help you become an influencer, but it is also just a great way to live.

People strive to pay their debts and return favors because no one likes to feel indebted, powerless or weak. This also means that we are more likely to do favors for people who offer them to us.

You also need to know what the people you are interacting with want. What drives them and what are their goals? What do they respond to most? Where are they finding value? In this way, you will be best able to see exactly what you can offer to set this reciprocal relationship in motion.

Action Item: Make a list of 5 to 10 of the most influential people in your industry and anyone else you generally want to align with. Then, write down a way to interact with each of them in a positive way. For example, you can send them all a creative gift or mention something specific you like about their work. This will get you on their radar and they will start paying attention to you.

Bill Rancic, a celebrity who was on the hit TV show *The Apprentice*, got his start by sending out funny glasses to the media in order to promote his cigar of the month club. Each time he sent out glasses to a new batch of media professionals, a handful would invite him on their show. By continuing in this way, he became a celebrity and an influencer in the business community.

Through his process of giving and getting in front of the media he made connections that resulted in his benefiting from their distribution. Each time he did this, his following grew a little more, and he received spikes in sales and revenue for his business. But it really led to much more than that; in the end, his repetitious media exposure led him to become the celebrity he is today.

To be an influencer, you must understand the business aspects of public relations and media. One small segment can double your influence and power. Rancic knew this and did an excellent job capitalizing on this knowledge. We will talk more about this point later in the book.

Commitment and Consistency

Humans perceive a deep connection between commitment and consistency. We look for consistency when we decide to commit and try to shape our commitments to conform to social norms and expectations.

Along these same lines, it is proven that the more someone sees you, the more they like you. Known as the mere-exposure effect, this psychological phenomenon is based on the evolutionary instinct to survive and thrive. In an article for *Psychology Today*, Dr. Raj Raghunathan explains that "familiar things – food, music, activities, surroundings, etc. – make us feel comfortable. Familiarity breeds liking. If something is familiar, we have clearly survived exposure to it, and our brain, recognizing this, steers us toward it."[3]

This plays a very, very important role in becoming an influencer. You must consistently get in front of the people you want to influence. The more time you spend and the more consistently you spend that time, the more you will be able to influence those people.

Whether your messaging is delivered through YouTube, blogging, Twitter, Facebook, Periscope (the most popular live streaming app online), television, email, etc., what matters is that you are regularly getting in

---

[3] Raghunathan, Raj, PhD. (2012). "Familiarity Breeds Enjoyment." *Psychology Today*. https://www.psychologytoday.com/blog/sapient-nature/201201/familiarity-breeds-enjoyment

front of your audience and delivering a consistent message. Human nature will then cause those people to conform and commit to you as an influencer, backing your messaging. In addition, they will share your ideas with others. Eventually, this process leads these followers marketing your work for you.

> **Action Item:** Think about developing an ongoing method to get in front of your audience. When they see you consistently over time, it will result in you having more influence in your space. Whether it is a weekly newsletter, video series, blog or event, this makes all the difference. Later, I'll give you a checklist of all the options. But for now, jot down a few ideas.

Social Proof

We humans feel safer in numbers – not just physically, but also socially. This is especially true when we feel threatened, anxious or unsure. This is why we seek out the ideas and opinions of others to guide our decision making. When that happens, we seek reassurance or social proof from others, especially people who seem trustworthy: influencers.

People care how many followers a business or person has and how many positive reviews or testimonials are readily available for viewing. Modern consumers love social proof and conform to it. They also care who makes these recommendations. The more influence you have, the more control you have over the consumer.

Does this mean we're all victims of peer pressure and blindly adhere to whatever influencers and consumer reviews tell us? No, not exactly. Here is the big difference.

Bowing to peer pressure has a negative feeling associated with it. It's the feeling of caving in under social pressure to either do something unwanted or to fail to do something desirable. Social proof is different from peer pressure. It offers the opposite feeling which is one of inclusion, i.e., being with the crowd that's doing the right thing. Following the social proof offered by an influencer is a positive action.

Consider these everyday examples of social proof creating influence:

- McDonald's tells everyone that billions and billions have been served;

- Laugh tracks are always used in situation comedies;

- Four out of five experts (doctors, dentists, whomever) agree that _____;

- At least 88% of us check online reviews as we shop, look for a place to eat, explore vacation destinations, and you name it.

Social proof is powerful, and influencers are masters of social proof. Why? Because they have their own social proof. In fact, they have established themselves to a degree that their own opinions *are* social proof. You cannot be an influencer without the support of social proof. You must have a large following on the channels that are most important to the people you influence.

> **Action Item:** Review the communities you have built on social media. Compare them to the top influencers in your industry. Where do you fall in regard to community size, targeted demographic and levels of interaction? Determine your top 5 strengths and top 5 weaknesses.

Liking

People we like or find likable are more likely to influence others. Maybe they're very kind or flattering, or maybe they "feel" like they are similar to us. Whatever the reason, we want to say "yes" to people we like.

This means that to be an influencer, others must like you. This is a complicated concept that operates on multiple levels.

Do you know Bill O'Reilly? If not, he is a tough-talking TV host and an influencer. He is also, generally, blunt and borderline rude. But people like and respect him for that, as people who follow him find that quality likable. In his own context, being blunt is seen as having more integrity and being unafraid to "buck the system."

This tells you that there are many reasons why people like a public figure. Not all public figures need to have obvious, more generally-accepted, likable qualities.

Related to this idea is that people say "yes" more readily to people with whom they have things in common, i.e., life experiences, family backgrounds and/or interests such as sports and hobbies. Keep this in mind, because when you are establishing your influencer persona and personal brand, you need to make sure you have things in common with your demographic. Align your principles so that you share ideas with those whom you want to influence.

Bill O'Reilly influences right wing Republicans. He has certain qualities that might not relate to the followers of an influencer like Kelly Slater, a main authority on surfing. Some of Kelly Slater's qualities are liberal, positive, easy going and drawn to environmental activism. Bill O'Reilly wears a suit every day; Kelly Slater's most common attire is sandals and board-shorts. Both influencers embody characteristics deemed likeable by their demographic.

To be likable, you need to invest your time and effort in building rapport and trust. You nurture good relationships with your co-workers, clients and others in the industry. You must do the same with the online communities you build.

You are reliable and consistent. You are an active listener who balances the knowledge that comes from experience with an open, creative mind that can innovate to find novel solutions.

You find genuine points of connection with others. Never fake it, but draw on your natural connections with other people. Are they a parent like you, or a soccer fan? Nail down all of the commonalities that you and your target demographic share, forging connections that way. As a small additional note, people generally like people more who they feel are attractive and who compliment them – in a sincere way.

You use your emotional intelligence (EI) to do all of these things because they work, and because you need genuine buy-in to be likable. No one likes a phony, and most people can spot them from a mile away. So when you create this influencer persona, do it out of the good of your heart, for the right reasons and to help people genuinely through your chosen business path. That confident guidance and the embodiment that you are doing business for the right reasons shine through and through.

Action Item: Create a list of all the main qualities your demographic has. If you have communities already, you can find great data in your Twitter, YouTube channel and Facebook business page analytics reports. You can also find data using tools such as FollowerWonk, Google Analytics Demographic and Interest Reports (you need to have this set up for your website to use it), BuzzSumo, QuantCast and Alexa. Take all this data and list out all of the qualities that you can find.

Take a critical look at yourself. Consider the points of alignment that you already share with your demographic. Decide which qualities in your demographic you need to enhance. Create a persona that your demographic will respect and follow. Make sure to touch on these points throughout your personal digital influencer marketing as your brand grows.

Authority

People are impressed by authority figures.

We believe they are more likely to possess expert knowledge and good judgment. Think Charlie Bolden, head of NASA. Inherently, based on his position, we adhere to his direction for all things space exploration. Clearly, he knows the field; he is the head of NASA.

People have an impulse to comply with authority because we experience a sense of obligation to authority figures. After all, you're an authority figure for a reason.

Along with authority comes respect. The trappings of success in your field and recognition from other influencers are powerfully persuasive to most.

As an influencer, you are an authority figure, but you also know how to leverage the authority of other powerful and influential individuals and institutions. You cannot simply say that you are great. You need to provide evidence and support for this claim.

Look at Tony Robbins who provides an

example of this. Robbins is a very well-known business advisor, life coach and speaker. He showcases these accomplishments on his Twitter profile in a factual way: "#1 New York Times best-selling author." In this way, he leverages the authority of *The New York Times* to support his own credibility and authority. This is the hook that attracts others into his sphere of influence.

Authority and credibility matter. This is why I recommend that you align with other influencers and sources of authority in order to further your influence. What are the main authorities in your industry? How can you get your name attached to them?

What sounds better?

> My name is John Lincoln, and I am the best digital marketing expert around. I am really good at SEO, social media, content marketing, analytics and conversion rate optimization. I have

helped a lot of people and businesses. Contact me now.

Or

John Lincoln, MBA, is CEO of Ignite Visibility and a digital marketing teacher at the University of California San Diego. Lincoln has worked with over 400 online businesses and has generated millions in revenue for clients. He is a noted author for Search Engine Land, Marketing Land, Search Engine Journal, Inc. Magazine and Entrepreneur Magazine and has been featured by Forbes, CIO Magazine, CMO Magazine, Good Morning San Diego, the Union Tribune, Business Insider and more. Lincoln has been awarded top conversion rate expert of the year, top SEO expert of the year, best social media campaign of the year, top marketing column of the year, top technology column of the year and top analytics column of the year. In 2014 and 2015, Ignite Visibility was named the #1 SEO company in California and one of the top two in the nation. Some of Lincoln's client's have been Fox, Coupons.com, USA Today, Jacuzzi, Links of London and more.

It's obvious, right?

This concept will become more important as we build your personal influencer brand. You need to have claims to fame that you can clearly state. This is very important because when new people get exposed to you online for the first time, there is a much greater chance they will join one of your online communities if you have a claim to fame – especially one that they'd love to have on their own resume.

Action Item: Create a bullet point list of everything positive you have accomplished in your business life. Did you increase revenue by 100%, publish a book, write a blog for a large publication, speak at an event, do an interview for someone, get a masters degree, help out an non-profit? Create a master list of everything you have done. Try to come up with the 20 best accomplishments of your career. Once you have your list send it to two to five people you trust. Ask them to rank all of your accomplishments 1 through 10. Now, take these top 10 accomplishments and make sure at least the top 3 are clear in each of your online profiles. If possible, add more.

General categories for this include the following. If you do not have an accomplishment in one of these categories, note that.

- Education
- Experience / Background
- Accomplishments
- Best Projects
- Recommendations
- Press
- Books
- Articles
- Awards

- Philanthropy

Scarcity

Things that are in limited supply hold more appeal for consumers. How would this make you feel? You are shopping for a TV and find the exact model you want on sale for $1! But there are 50 other people waiting at the front door to get the same TV, too! You would most-likely feel a burning desire to get that TV before the rest of the group.

Scarcity is based not only in psychology, but in the basic theories of economics: supply and demand control scarcity and perceived value. This is the impetus that causes people to line up outside a store for hours to get the next big thing.

The concept of scarcity when applied to consumer behavior causes us to feel that we may miss out on an experience, service or product. We want the product or service that is in limited supply because no one likes the feeling of losing or being left out.

As an influencer, you are, in fact, a resource which is in limited supply and for which there is a growing demand. This means you do not want to over-communicate. You want your communication to be deliberate and have a meaningful impact each time. By doing this, it will leave your followers wanting more. They will wait for your next message and jump on it. My wife has a great saying for this: "Don't be desperate." I strongly support and adhere to this concept; share your thoughts and perspective only when you truly have something valuable to add to the conversation. Moreover, any sense to desperation in communication always causes followers to lose interest.

> **Action Item:** Review the top five most influential people in your industry. Check out their social profiles and communities and get a feel for how often they update their communities on industry activities and what methods they use to communicate with their audience. See where they have the

highest engagement rates and what posts are less effective in terms of comments and level of response. Notice the type of content they are posting and note the frequency and length of their communications.

How You Can Use Targeted Content to Grow Your Influence

So far, we've learned about the different types of influencers out there, as well as the science behind influence. This section will dive into strategic and actionable items that you can use to begin establishing yourself as an influencer – one of them being content marketing.

What is content marketing? According to the Content Marketing Institute, *"Content marketing is a strategic marketing approach focused on creating and distributing valuable, relevant, and consistent content to attract and retain a clearly-defined audience – and, ultimately, to drive profitable customer action."*

In a nutshell, content marketing is creating content on topics that surround your industry so that you can be seen as an authority and attract business. Content can be anything from videos to presentations to articles to images and more.

In the online space, content marketing is so important to building a following.

You really have to be deliberate and focus on quality. Little tweaks mean the difference between you or your competitor becoming an influencer because it is extremely competitive.

Each month, I publish 12 articles on the Ignite Visibility University Blog and four to eight columns or blogs around the web. This results in new people finding out about me and getting new content in front of current followers. As a result, this drives more business to our website and grows influencer status.

But before you go and start publishing at this scale, there is a lot you need to know. So let's get started.

Find Your Voice

Finding your public voice and using it is key. This is the voice you will use for online content, social media, videos and even public speaking.

Remember these basic truths as you find your voice:

Control Your Message and Demeanor. Practice doing this so it becomes second nature to you. I often tell people that you actually *do* need to fake it until you make it.

In a recent Ted Talk, social psychologist Amy Cuddy explained how she proved that "power posing"– standing in a posture of confidence, even when we don't feel confident – can affect testosterone and cortisol levels in the brain, and might even have an impact on our chances for success.

The longer you practice and model something, the more it actually becomes you. If you are young and getting your start, being nervous and intimidated is very normal. Fake it until you make it, and one day you will wake up and realize: I am who I have been striving to be.

Be Expressive and Show Genuine Feelings. Practice saying just what you mean; don't beat around the bush. It wastes time, feels annoying, and makes you seem insincere even if you're not. If you are going to be an influencer, you must be confident enough to be real and direct.

Show Sensitivity to Others. Listen to people, and you'll know how to respond. The more you hear, the more complete your sense of their needs and habits will be. By listening to the needs of your industry, it will also give you ideas for where you as an influencer can address topics, thus further propelling your voice.

Be Nice. Don't run all over other people just

trying to gain influence. Be the best version of yourself that you can be to attain influence. Don't be petty or pick fights; play the long game. Every person you meet in your life has the potential to be a connection that can benefit you, so don't do anything to risk alienating people. Finally, know that there will be people who are rude, mean and try to bring you down constantly. Ignore them. You need to develop thick skin if you want to be an influencer.

> **Action Item:** Develop brand standards for your own persona. Create an outline of your messaging and include specific ways you can deal with conflict. This is particularly useful because eventually, when you get big enough, you will need to hire other people to help manage your personal brand who will need this information. However, even if you do not reach this level for some time, having your core values and brand standards in one place provides a good check and balance for your own guidance and consistency.

Action Item: Create a bullet point list of things you would never say or do online. Examples might be to post a curse word, talk down to someone or mention a specific industry topic (for example, I try to never talk about politics online). Choose thoughtfully and stick to this list.

Find Your Focus

An influencer must choose and master a specific area within an industry. No one can be an expert on every detail of your entire industry, and if your focus is too broad, you will neither gain the right expertise to function nor be perceived as an authority. People expect an authority to have a much deeper understanding of a topic than they have, so focus is critical. The less focused you are, the less you can influence within a particular niche.

Start with the basics of your focus area and master them by researching, theorizing, experimenting and expanding the subject.

This is exactly what I have done over the last decade or so when blogging, and I recommend you do the same. You'll learn amazing amounts of information as you do this, but just as importantly, you'll be seen within your niche over and over again. Your name and face will become part of the fabric of your focus area.

As you hone your theories and learn new things, you'll gain a deeper understanding of your focus area. Your goal will be to move from reading and restating the ideas of others to generating your own. If possible, never read and restate at all, only publish content with a twist or expansion. Remember this key point: your content must be different and unique in some way.

> **Action Item:** List the top five to ten most exciting and innovative topics in your industry. Consider which ones will have the brightest futures and most longevity. Select two to five of these topics to make the core of your writing. Pick the ones you love, where you can

be an authority and where you can attract the right type of business. For example, I write on conversion rate optimization, SEO, social media, analytics and content marketing.

Choose the Right Topics and Focus Them

When it comes to actually creating content for online marketing there is a lot to know, and some industries are really competitive in this channel. Generally, it is a good idea to choose niche topics that target the type of business you want to attract. You can also choose broad topics, but if you do, yours needs to be the best article on the subject, so you need to invest more time in the content creation.

Here is the rule: the more focused in a niche the topic is, the less competitive it is (usually), and fewer people are seeking that information. The broader the topic is, the more competitive it is, and many more people are seeking that information. In addition, for a broader topic, your content needs to cover more aspects of the topic so the user gets what they are looking for.

Here is a real world example. In 2013, I wrote a post on multilingual and multi-regional SEO for Search Engine Land. When I wrote that post, I could have stopped at 500 words, but instead, I turned it into the ultimate guide on the topic. This post ended up being thousands of words and now ranks number one in Google for terms like multilingual SEO, SEO multilingual and multi language SEO.

That post has turned into a consistent form of leads for our business and has resulted in hundreds of thousands of dollars in revenue for our business. People read the post, see our company as an authority on international SEO and hire us.

My multilingual and multi-regional SEO piece is an example of a broad topic which tens of thousands of other articles have covered in some way. It is substantial and comprehensive, though, so it became the number one piece of content on the topic.

Ten Key Points

1. Remember: each topic you choose should be tempting enough to get busy people to read the first few lines.
2. Create unique content that highlights your brand and ideas.
3. Don't stop at finding merely great topics; identify unusual, compelling angles you could take on topics that your audience is interested in.
4. Write on everything in the universe around the services or products you provide.
5. Align your content with your target audience's interests and needs.
6. Use your expertise and insight to solve their problems, answer their questions, and entertain them in specific and meaningful ways.
7. Make people see you as a resource on the subject.
8. Take complicated issues and transform them into compact, easily understood,

usable content for your readers.

9. Engage in competitive analysis before you create your content. Search using your working title and see what's out there. Make sure you compile the best piece of content on the topic.

10. Read content that's on point to identify what's missing or left unsaid, and then focus your content to bridge the gap.

This is where you really highlight your authority − you take what's out there and go beyond it. Bridge the gaps between existing resources. Fold in your own insights based on your expertise and experience. In this way, your content is relevant yet unique and adds value.

Your brand and value proposition also become your long-term goal; everything you do must make sense within that paradigm. For example, my business mission is to "help others through digital marketing." Our core company values are honesty, hard work, innovation, over-delivering for clients and growing their business and results.

Action Item: Take a moment and think about your business mission and values. List your main goal in business in a few sentences. What is the main goal that drives you every day?

Optional Action Item: Take your business mission, your life mission and your main goals. Add the goals to the notifications on your smart phone alarm (I like using the app ColorNote for this). When your alarm turns on every morning, you will be reminded of your goals. For example, when my alarm turns on in the morning I get the following message. "Some are afraid to die; others are afraid not to fully live. Seize the day, push boundaries, break barriers and fully live and love those around you." I also get these reminders: "Be a good husband and dad. Appreciate it. Trust in GD. Stay true to mission to help others through marketing. Don't work too early or too late. Exercise, Be Present." When you get this reminder everyday in the morning, it sinks in. My mission does not need to be your mission. But this process will help you stay focused.

Chapter 2: Becoming an Influencer

This chapter will cover the many ways you can become an influencer online through content creation and marketing. I'll cover the different ways you can create compelling content through blogging, guest posting, SEO, social media and more. I'll also provide tips and give examples of how to pitch industry blogs and news publications for publishing your content. We'll discuss generating article topics and using infographics, videos and white papers as well.

How to Gain Influence Through Blogging

You absolutely need to blog to be an authority in your industry. You must stay organized, and plan your blogging so that you will publish consistently. Generally, WordPress is the best platform for blogging and for any basic website. Now, there is a difference between WordPress.com and the WordPress content management system.

Wordpress.com is a website where you can set up a blog in minutes online. That is not what you want to do.

What you want to do is to have a blog that lives on your main website on a directory structure. That means if your website is www.example.com, you will be able to find your blog at www.example.com/blog. This will ensure your blog is seen by search engines and users as part of your main site.

There are many other ways to build blogs online. Almost all major website builders like ExpressionEngine, Drupal, Joomla, SquareSpace, Shopify, Magento, etc., either have a blogging feature or the ability to add one.

However, there is a reason why WordPress is used by 59% of websites online; it's simple, intuitive and flexible. When it comes to hosting your blog, I recommend wpengine.com. They do an excellent job.

So now it is time to blog. Aim for a minimum

of two posts per week. Of course, the more you publish the more blog traffic you will create, and an increase in the frequency of blogging will grow your following faster. Use an editorial calendar to stay on track and stick to it.

It is proven that in general longer blog posts rank better in search engines, get more shares and have more longevity. Try to shoot for blog posts between 1,000 and 5,000 words (2,000 to 3,000 words is the sweet spot right now). However, the more competitive the topic, the more complete the post needs to be.

Your blog content must be valuable and usable. It must be in line with your expertise and your search engine optimization strategy (we will cover SEO later). Its purpose is to show who you are and allow you to disseminate your knowledge. Your blog is your voice in the world.

There is so much to know about how to blog, so before you start a blog, talk with an expert about how to maximize the reach of your blog. Otherwise, you could be blogging for no reason.

I have written hundreds of posts on blogging and have read just as many. I recommend reading the posts below before you start. I have written some of these posts, and others are from respected experts around the web. You don't have to do this now. But make a note to read them before you start a blog. It will save you time, money and worlds of frustration.

1. "The 6 Biggest Mistakes in Corporate Blogging" (Marketing Land)
2. "How to Grow Your Blog to 100,000 Visits Per Month in 18 Months" (QuickSprout)
3. "How To Harness the Marketing Power of Blogs" (Entrepreneur)
4. "How to Write a Blog that Drives Traffic and Sales" (Ignite Visibility)
5. "5 Creative Tips to Help Increase Blog Traffic and Boost Your Business" (Social Media Examiner)
6. "Increase Traffic to Your Site with

These Tried and True Blogging Tips" (WPMU Dev)
7. "How To Write Magnetic Headlines" (CopyBlogger)
8. "The SEO and User Science Behind Long-Form Content" (Search Engine Land)

Action Item: Make plans to do the following.

- Add a WordPress blog to your website on a directory structure.
- Before you start to blog, read posts 1-8 above. Remember, blogging is competitive so you need to know your stuff first.
- Come up with a list of your main themes and then develop three months' worth of article topics, infographic topics, video topics and white papers around them.

Secrets to Guest Posting Like a Pro

The majority of the time, it is more beneficial to publish your blog on another website besides your own.

Guest posting allows you to reach a whole new community. It further establishes you as an expert and brings people to your blog. Strive to make your guest posts even better than your everyday content. Think of it like public speaking at an event, except without the nerves!

The hardest part about guest blogging is getting your foot in the door. But after you have written for someone once, it is very easy to do it again. Also, once you write for one website, others will want you to write for them, too.

Here is how I did it.

I started off blogging on a company blog. After I wrote about 50 solid posts, I crafted a pitch and emailed a few blogs. The pitch looked something like this.

Hi there,

My name is John Lincoln and I really want to be your next columnist. I am a major fan of the publication and I especially liked the recent article you published on <>. I am 100% dedicated to writing quality content for you and I would be a perfect fit. Articles on time, fully edited and innovative.

Here is my bio:
[Short bio goes here]
Here are examples of my work:
[Links to author bios and top articles go here]

Here are the first 5 topics I would like to write on:
[5 article topics go here]

Here are my social media profiles:
[Facebook profile < - Number of followers
YouTube channel <- Number of followers

Twitter profile <- Number of followers]

Is there an article I can start on for you now? Just let me know what topic you like best.

Thank you,

John

Now, the hard part is not crafting the pitch; the hard part is finding the right person to reach out to. Also, you need to know your limits.

If you have a relationship with someone, and they have a blog, write a post. You have to provide the guest blogs for free, complete with images, but it is worth it for the exposure and a link to your website and to get in front of their audience.

It is a good idea to start with small blogs first. For example, I started off guest blogging on other companies' blogs, smaller news blogs and really anyone who would take a post.

Generally, it is a good idea to work with people you know. Over time, this process led to establishing a large portfolio of guest blogs. This, in turn, allowed me to craft better and better pitches. Eventually, my hard work paid off and led to writing for Search Engine Land, Marketing Land, Inc. Magazine and Entrepreneur magazine.

Finding Guest Posting Opportunities

So, how do you find places to write? While it is best to approach sites of friends or business partners, or industry sites you are aware of first, there are other methods. For example, here is a big list of 36 places I have developed that you can pitch anytime (https://ignitevisibility.com/best-places-guest-blog/). But these are not the right places for everyone and if you are just getting started you will probably not be accepted.

Simple searching is another great method. It is a good idea to search for places that are industry specific. Here is how that works.

If you're looking for something online, where do you usually go? Probably Google. Your efforts to find guest posting opportunities should be no exception to this rule.

Go to Google and type in a search string that will return sites that allow people to guest post. If you're not sure which strings to use, don't worry, because I've provided them right here:

- submit a guest post
- guest post by
- accepting guest posts
- want to write for us
- guest post guidelines
- guest post opportunities
- this is a guest post by
- submit blog post
- contribute to our site
- guest column
- submit content
- submit your content
- submit post
- guest post courtesy of
- submit an article

- contributor guidelines
- guest posts wanted

Keep in mind that all of these keyword search phrases will land you on sites that offer guest posting opportunities for a variety of subjects, some of which may have nothing to do with your niche. That's okay, though. You either need to get creative and find a way to offer some valuable content to those sites or move on to one that is more in your niche.

You can enhance every single keyword search phrase in the list above by adding a niche-relevant keyword at the front of it and then performing the search. For example, if the keyword you're trying to rank for is "blue widgets," then you would type "blue widgets submit a post" into the Google search bar. That should give you a list of sites specific to your keyword and that also accept guest posts.

In most cases, you'll find that you need to contact the webmaster to request a guest post opportunity. That's usually not a problem, since almost every website has a "Contact" link in the header or footer nowadays. Someone checks that message, so make sure you send your best pitch through that channel.

In other cases, the webmaster will provide you with a user interface that allows you to submit an article on the spot. For example, websites such as Medium.com and Buzzfeed.com allow you to guest blog just by creating an account.

Competitive Analysis for Guest Posting

You'll find that some competitors and peers list all their media coverage or columns. By doing a little competitive analysis and seeing where the top influencers in your industry have guest blogged, you can find opportunities for yourself.

Start by picking the top ten people in your industry. Google their names individually along with terms like *column, article, guest post, author* or *profile*. This will return almost all the places they have ever written online. Their social media profiles are especially valuable, because if they wrote a post somewhere, they probably shared it on Twitter or Facebook. This means you can discover the same opportunities for yourself just by reviewing their feeds. You can then take this information and organize it in an excel sheet or Google sheet and pitch the same publications.

You can also just search on Twitter in general. Go to Twitter and perform a search on *guest post, author, feature, column,* etc. That will give you a list of tweets by people who are bragging about a recent guest post. Even better, enter your keyword plus *guest post* (i.e., *blue widgets guest post*) to see niche-related results.

The great thing about performing a Twitter search is that your top results will typically be only a few minutes to a few hours old. That will give you a great opportunity to reach out to webmasters which are currently accepting guest posts.

Perform the same searches on LinkedIn. You might find even more opportunities. I use LinkedIn often for this, and it works well. Both in the general LinkedIn feed and the group feeds, you will see people talking about the latest post they had published.

There are a few things you should remember about social media in this context. Most of the people managing focused social media accounts or public figure social media accounts for a business also manage the blog. If you need a contact for guest blogging, start by messaging a business account on Twitter, Facebook, etc., and ask there first.

For example, I know that in the digital marketing industry almost all of the agency and software social profiles are also managed by the person who manages the blog (and if they don't, they probably sit next to the person who does at the office). If I want to guest post somewhere, I can Tweet to them and ask.

This brings up another point. Don't think that having to ask lessens your influence, or that "real" influencers don't have to ask to guest post because they're so well known. In reality, just the opposite is true! Influencers who know what they're doing reach out to people every day.

Another thing to keep in mind is that most people guest blog so they can get links to their website. If you use a backlink analysis tool, you can see all the links pointing at someone else's site. A large percentage of those will typically be guest blog posts.

Fire up your backlink tracker of choice (Moz Open Site Explorer is an excellent option, as is Majestic Site Explorer) and plug in your competitor's domain. Then, view the backlinks to the site. Look for possibilities of guest posting through the list that gets returned.

This option requires a little more effort than the others, but you could come across some great guest posting opportunities on established blogs if you take advantage of it.

Important Guest Posting Tips I've Learned through Experience

If you want to guest post for a big publication, don't reach out without doing your homework. Research their submission guidelines, read some articles and familiarize yourself with their themes. Craft your pitch carefully, and make sure to pitch a piece that covers something new for them or expands significantly on what they've already posted.

You only get one chance to pitch an editor for a contributor section in a major national or international publication so do plenty of research. Also, make sure you are pitching the right person; if you aren't, you may be wasting time for months and never even get a reply.

As you seek out guest posting opportunities, remember that you often need to give before you receive. There needs to be something in it for them. They already create a lot of excellent content, so show them why it's worth the time to let you post that content instead.

Present an amazing bio and a one-of-a-kind topic. Tell them something positive you will do for them, such as offer them a glowing review of their service (if it is a company site) or improve on a topic for a news site. Make sure to tell them you will share the post with your thousands of followers (we will teach you how to get thousands of followers later), link to the post from your website or even give them a product sample.

When you approach a place to guest blog, put yourself in the blog editor's shoes. What makes them tick? They have likes, interests and goals. For example, I love to surf, play soccer, and I want to build traffic to our website. So if you knew that about me you could pitch me by saying:

Hi John,

I noticed you are a big surfer and went to UC Santa Cruz. I love surfing in Santa Cruz. The waves are amazing! Did you surf much while you were there in college? I sent you a Santa Cruz hat in the mail as small thanks for considering my email. I am a big fan of your work at <insert magazine>.

I am reaching out to you because I have a post that is going to generate a lot of traffic for your site. The post is…

Now you don't need to buy them a hat (of course it wouldn't hurt). But you get the idea. If you lead in with something like this, you started off on the right foot and I would be much more willing to help you. I love to surf, I love Santa Cruz, and I want to help other people who are like-minded. Editors really appreciate someone going the extra mile while at the same time not being too over the top or desperate.

Know that larger publications take a lot longer to reach. They are being pitched by thousands of people a day. It is best if you have a unique angle or a connection when you approach them. I recommend using LinkedIn to see if you know anyone the main editor knows before pitching him or her. If you have a common acquaintance or a similar interest, it will help you get noticed, so mention the mutual acquaintance or interest when you reach out.

It generally takes three to nine months to become a writer or to be mentioned in a major publication. You also need to at least have some basic credentials. I pitched Inc. Magazine five times and waited for six months before they got back to me. I also mailed them my personal information and pitch directly. You can read more about what it takes to write for large publications by reading this article at Forbes (http://www.forbes.com/sites/susannahbreslin/2011/04/06/how-to-become-a-forbes-blogger/).

Smaller blogs are the easiest to get placements on. When I am approaching a smaller site, I generally like to provide them with a piece of content that is so good, it is very hard to say no to. Bigger publications want the pitch, and they want to approve the topic. Smaller publications and company blogs just need good content. Remember: no matter what, it cannot be promotional content for your company. It needs to fit with their theme.

It is fine to treat editors as you would a prospect; you just can't pay directly to be published. If you do, that needs to be labeled as an advertorial or sponsored post – which is okay, but is also slightly different. Make sure to read the FTC guidelines on social media and blogging: https://www.ftc.gov/tips-advice/business-center/guidance/ftcs-endorsement-guides-what-people-are-asking[4]

Action Item: Create a Google Sheet or Excel Sheet and develop a list of 40 to

---

[4] Federal Trade Commission (May 2015). *The FTC's Endorsement Guides: What People are Asking.* https://www.ftc.gov/tips-advice/business-center/guidance/ftcs-endorsement-guides-what-people-are-asking

50 places where you would like to guest blog. Think of friends' websites, strategic partners' websites, industry sites, regional publications and national publications (where are your customers?). Take it upon yourself or have someone on your team find the contact information for each of the publications. Rank them from difficult to easy to write for. Craft a universal pitch that will work for each of them. Come up with 3 unique article topics for each publication. Pitch 2 publications a week and make sure to follow up with each publication at least 6 times before giving up. Keep track of all of your work and build on your sheet over time. Aim to get anywhere between 1 and 4 guest blogs written and published on other sites each month. Use this process to continue to build your portfolio and your distribution.

How You Can Use SEO to Drive Your Authority

Search engine optimization is a large and complicated topic. I have taught four-day courses on it at UCSD and still do not cover everything. Also, it is an industry that is constantly evolving at a rapid pace. So I will just give you the basics of what you need in this section.

All influencers need to have their main website optimized, target a variety of terms in their blog posts, and be consistently contributing to a set of keywords that relate to their top themes. I recommend you read the Google starter guide before doing an SEO for your site (http://static.googleusercontent.com/media/www.google.com/en/webmasters/docs/search-engine-optimization-starter-guide.pdf).

You can also learn everything you need to know by following one or more of these news outlets:

- Search Engine Land
- Marketing Land
- Search Engine Journal

- Google Webmaster Central Blog
- Moz Blog
- Ignite Visibility Blog
- Quick Sprout Blog

SEO gets technical, so if this section is a little over your head, you may want to speak with your website developer about these items or hire an SEO expert. Also, if you have any questions you can always tweet directly to me @johnelincoln

Core Tools

When you get started with SEO for your website, you need to start by setting up Google Search Console and Google Analytics. Make sure you take the time to install those tools.

Technical Checklist

Next, make sure you have a robots.txt file, XML sitemap and HTML sitemap at a minimum. You want to put a hyperlink to your HTML sitemap in your footer so that Google can find all your pages when crawling your site.

Research Your Keywords

Next, do some keyword research. The two best tools for this are SEM Rush and the Google Keyword Planner Tool. The Google Keyword Planner Tool is free, and although SEM Rush charges, it offers a great deal of competitive data. Drop your competitors' websites into SEM Rush and get lots of data you can use to optimize your site.

Usc thcsc tools to develop a list of the top terms you want to rank for. Remember, SEO is very competitive, so keep the keywords that work within your niche and make sure they are terms that are actually possible. Also, it is generally a good idea to start local and branch out from there.

For example, when we first started Ignite Visibility we optimized the site for *SEO company San Diego*, *social media company San Diego*, and *internet marketing company San Diego*. Once we nailed our local rankings down, we started expanding nationally. Develop a list of ten keywords to start and three to five keywords that support each of those main keywords.

Optimize Your Site

Assign 3 to 5 keywords to each page on your site. An example would look like this:

Surfboards San Diego
Best Surfboards San Diego
San Diego High Performance Surfboards
Buy Longboard Surfboards in San Diego

The first keyword is your main keyword and is your best bet. Work the first keyword into the following items for each page:

- Page title
- Meta Description
- h1
- h2
- Image file name
- Image alt text
- Copy

Make sure there are at least 500 words of copy, and mention the first two keywords on your list two to three times within those 500 words. Use the remaining keywords once in the 500 words of copy.

Create Your Top Pages

For each keyword that makes sense for a standalone page, create a new page. For example, you would create distinct pages for different brands such as *Rusty Surfboards* and *Channel Island Surfboards*.

Blog on Your Top Areas

When you used the keyword tool, it probably gave you a lot of terms that you would like to rank for but did not make sense in terms of having its own page. These keywords are perfect to target in your blog posts. Blog on those topics as well as your top keyword terms that may have their own pages. Using the surfing term as an example, here are some possible posts:

- The Ultimate Guide to Channel Island Surfboards in 2016
- Rusty Surfboards: How to Select the Perfect Shape and Size
- Epoxy Surfboards: Everything You Need to Know

By writing on the terms associated with your keywords, you will be seen as an expert in those subjects and eventually rank for them.

Build Up Content in Your Top Areas

It is very important to organize your content correctly on your website. By aggregating content and building up hubs (areas of your site that list all the content you have on a topic), your page will rank better. Make sure to take everything you have written and list the titles on one page. Using the Channel Island Surfboards example, you can take all those articles and list them on the main Channel Islands page on your website. This shows both users and search engines that you know your stuff.

Build Links and Shares by Growing

Distribution, Advertising and PR

Try to get links from authoritative websites whenever you can; this is one of your most important SEO tasks. The more high-quality links you make, the better you will rank. Get listed on all of the top sites in your industry so you can link back to your website. The best things you can do in this area are guest blogging, great PR and writing so much high-quality content that people start to link to you naturally.

> **Action Item**: Make sure to follow the steps above for your own website. If you do not understand the SEO side, speak with your SEO company, developer or Tweet to me @johnelincoln.

Be Innovative, Have Something to Say, Get Listened To

Malcolm Gladwell wrote in his book *Outliers* that you need 10,000 hours of work, education and experience in your area to gain the true expertise of a world-class performer.[5]

Which topics have you invested yourself in to that degree? Which compel you enough that you hope to spend 10,000 hours on them? If you have not put in the time, it could be hard to be a true influencer in an industry.

You may worry that focusing your work within a niche limits you, but I can tell you that some of my most successful clients have really focused and owned a niche. Once you own that niche and are profitable, you can always expand into complementary markets.

Create a Feed So Your Knowledge is Cutting-Edge

Read case studies, expert articles and news that the influencers in your industry share. Look for news alerts and press releases about your key subject matter areas. And don't forget sources like industry magazines and specialty news outlets. Influencer status

---

[5] Gladwell, Malcolm. *Outliers: The Story of Success*, reprint edition. New York City, Back Bay Books: 2011.

requires you to be in the know.

But how can you possibly stay on top of all of that? Use feed tools. Feedly and tools like it allow you to follow a sizable variety of blogs, alerts and other sources of information.

I get most of my news through Twitter, email newsletters I subscribe to, YouTube videos and a few core websites. Make sure you have a constant feed of information coming to you from the best online sources. Take 30 minutes to 1 hour every day to study what is new.

Social media dashboards like Hootsuite and TweetDeck also help you keep track of lots of moving parts so you can watch various streams that matter to your online work.

Finally, never underestimate the value of a good Twitter list, which is a way to organize people you follow on Twitter based on your own preferences. For example, I have a Twitter list for media contacts, SEO people, content marketers, employees, etc. From the personal education perspective, a Twitter list can allow you to organize all your favorite news sites and editors in one place. This helps with education, finding shareable content and outreach.

> **Action Item**: Develop a list of all the best blogs, news sites, YouTube channels and publishers in your industry. Subscribe to each of the sites via email or by an RSS feed. Try to subscribe to at least ten of the top sites. Set aside 30 minutes to 1 hour each day to read what is new. Keep in mind, these may also be the sites you try to guest blog for, so learn the topics, authors and editors inside and out. It will help you throughout your career.

Communicate Publically

Why send an influencer an email when you can Tweet them and start a public conversation? Each time you seek engagement this way you have the potential to gain new followers.

Find the influencer you want to connect with and follow them. Tweet a message to them with a link that mentions them and ask a question or comment on their recent work. If you have comments about products or services, Tweet them and show you know your business.

If you really want to connect with someone, mention them on your blogs or in social media over and over again. Eventually, they will not be able to ignore it. When an influencer responds to you publically, their followers will see that they mentioned you, and it will add to your credibility and following.

Hashtag Research

A hashtag is a way to organize information by theme. When you add a hashtag on sites like Twitter, it makes it so that your message is added to the channel for that hashtag. For example, if I do #socialmedia, everyone looking at the #socialmedia feed will see that content.

For this reason, it is important to identify which Twitter hashtags are most frequently used by people in your industry. You need to know because your hashtag-laden tweets draw two groups: your followers, of course, but also anyone searching for that term.

Search for content using the hashtags that are most relevant to your work. When you find great content this way, share it with the hashtag that helped you find it and with other relevant hashtags. If research like this isn't getting you everything you want, use Hashtagify. It offers great insight into the best hashtags.

Verify whether your strategy is working once you've established and followed your plan by using Klout to see where you rank within social media influencer circles. Klout ranks users based on how consistent they are with content sharing, how responsive they are to engagement, and what they should be doing better. There is some controversy around Klout and its scores, but I generally like it.

Why and How You Need to Educate Others

Education is always multi-directional. As you continue to educate yourself, educate others in many different venues. Influencers must be constantly creating ways to educate others.

Schedule speaking engagements and present at conferences. Even within your niche you can add value in a variety of settings, so research carefully and find out what all of your options are. The other presenters you meet there will be part of an incredibly rich resource network.

Create and run seminars and webinars. This takes a lot of energy, but you can also charge for them, so you are educating and engaging while gaining financially.

Webinars are especially cost-effective because you can record and reuse them. Tools like Stealth Seminars make this very easy. You can also use GoToWebinar or even do a live event on a site like Periscope or Meerkat.

Send press releases in addition to your normal social media activities. If you don't know how to write them correctly − and this is a specific skill − learn how or hire someone to write them. News and industry outlets should be able to see right away what the press release is about, and they should also be able to grab images and a ready-to-print article using the press release so the work they need to put in is minimal.

Create or participate in radio shows, internet radio shows, or podcasts. You can do this solo or take the opportunity to invite influencers in your field for a better show and a joint promotional opportunity.

There are great software packages and apps for each online format. BlogTalk Radio allows you to set up an internet radio show or podcast quickly, distributing and syndicating your content so it is immediately available everywhere. Audacity is another excellent tool for beginners wanting to create podcasts.

Create informational products like guides, e-books, and even traditional books. Once you have amassed multiple successful articles, combine them into a book. Turn a shorter post or series into an educational handbook or how-to.

Influencers educate others and offer them actionable advice. Your reader should walk away with new ideas, questions, solutions, and plans. Let them have something really unique and valuable – that's what experts do. Give it all away, and if you are really that good, the business will come back to you ten-fold.

Action Item: Create a list of ten topics that you can use for webinars, live events, press releases and general media outreach. What are some new topics and angles that you can cover which others have not?

Know Your Audience Like the Backside of Your Hand

To create truly compelling, engaging content, you have to know your audience. Know who they are, what they care about and why they care.

Understand their behaviors, beliefs, careers, families and lifestyles. Let that understanding guide you as you think about what they want and need as if you were shopping for a gift for a loved one; imagine what they would be excited to see.

Enjoy the feeling that you will be giving people something they want and use it to motivate yourself.

> **Action Item**: Study the people who influence you as well as the other influencers in your industry. Watch what they do on social media, what they share and how they interact with others. Create your own model and improve on what

they do. By going through this exercise, you will further enhance your understanding of your own audience, find out what their pain points are and give them what they need to solve those issues.

How to Befriend Influencers and Leverage Each Other

To establish yourself as an influencer, you need to interact with other influencers. Find their best work; share and promote it. Thank them if they do the same, and when they thank you, start the conversation. You may not get a response from very famous influencers by promoting their work (since so many do it) but those who are on the rise like you will often answer you.

It can be a good idea to find an area where a current influencer is struggling and connect with them there. For example, say they are trying to grow their LinkedIn following but already have huge numbers on Twitter and Facebook. Comment on their LinkedIn articles and let them know you love them. They will notice. This all goes back to helping others. If their motivation is to get more LinkedIn comments, give them that. They will want to help you in return.

Focus your effort and time on the right influencers for your industry, and be persistent, without being a stalker. Your connections with influencers speak volumes about your brand and raise your professional credibility.

The other day, I wrote a post that was retweeted and praised by the head of SEO at Yahoo. This is a perfect example of someone in the space whom I was very happy to learn enjoyed my post. Over time, I have developed relationships with almost all of the top people in my industry through this process. You can do the same.

Research influencers in your industry so you can target those that can help you – and be helped by you. Create a list of influencers you want to reach, and work on it over time.

Make a Twitter list and keep track of what they do. Interact with them, study their work, help them and replicate similar or better work for yourself.

Start interacting and keep trying. Eventually, as you grow as an influencer and continue to help others and interact with them, you will build a relationship.

Some of the best tools for finding influencers are BuzzSumo, FollowerWonk and Klout. Each of these tools allows you to determine who the most powerful people in a space are. I'll dive into tools more in a moment.

Action Item: Test out BuzzSumo, FollowerWonk and Klout.com. Sign up for the websites and use them to determine the top 30 influencers in your industry. Save that information in a Google sheet so that you can reach out to these people in the future and build relationships. Create a Twitter list with these people on it. Interact with them once a week.

Engage via Social Media

To become an influencer, you must share your ideas and be seen. Answer questions on Quora, participate in and lead Tweet Chats and Google Plus hangouts. And use social media for when you can't attend something in person.

Social media offers you the chance not just to act as an influencer, but to be seen influencing. This may seem like a subtle distinction, but it isn't. If no one sees you in your influencer role, how much impact can you be having?

It's always a good idea to be present, but being present in the moment from a viral standpoint requires social media. If you miss viral moments, you can't influence; if you're not in on the conversation, you definitely can't lead it.

Watch for comments on your post and use those openings for more interaction. Don't shut down the conversation; ask open-ended questions to prompt more engagement.

As an influencer, you must know exactly how social media channels will best work for your brand.

Upon which platform are your industry leaders most often active? Choose that one to be your primary platform and publish there several times every day.

If you're not sure which platforms are strongest in your industry, do competitive research and see where your competition is doing well.

Part of truly high-quality engagement is really listening. Yes, you need to have something to say, but this is only half of the conversation.

People love to be listened to, this is a universal truth. Someone with authority and influence who still listens to others holds a tremendous amount of power.

It's easy to get wrapped up in your own ideas and problems; we all do it at times. Just remember that this absolutely cannot be your day-to-day MO. Social media should not be the place where you air your grievances with the world or blurt out whatever is on your mind without thinking. Once it's out there, it's there forever and part of your online persona.

Social Media Sites You Should be Looking At

Social media is absolutely essential for marketers, and influencers are masters of this marketing channel. But social media isn't a no-brainer. There are many platforms out there, and together, they comprise a complex web of options.

Most business owners and aspiring influencers tend to be focused on one controlling issue: which platforms are best to use and why? I have invested most of my time in Twitter, YouTube, Facebook and LinkedIn. These have been great avenues for our business, and we currently get new clients from each social media site monthly.

To best make these decisions, you must know where your audience is spending its time.

Just as critical to your social media success is your ability to understand the nuances of each platform. Here are my top social media sites that you should be taking a second look at.

Most Important Social Media Websites

Below are the top social media sites you should be looking at for participation based on your demographic.

Facebook

With more than 1.3 billion users − almost half of them active on a daily basis − Facebook is the largest social network in the world.[6] On average, each Facebook user has 130 friends and is connected to 80 community pages,

---

[6] Jones, Kelsey (November 15, 2013). "The Growth of Social Media, version 2.0." *Search Engine Journal.* https://www.searchenginejournal.com/growth-social-media-2-0-infographic/77055/

groups and events.[7]

No matter what your area of expertise, it is very likely that a large part of your audience is on Facebook. Facebook gives you a place to engage and connect with people in order to transform them into customers and followers; it also helps you build your brand and drive traffic with targeted ads and great data. Influencers commonly create a business page for themselves like this: *https://www.facebook.com/johnlincolnofficial*

Twitter

All influencers need a Twitter profile because Twitter is one of the easiest ways for anyone to connect with influencers and celebrities. The average user has more than 200 followers and spends almost three hours on the platform every day – that's a huge amount of time for you to grab their attention.

Twitter is strongest as a place to build brand

[7] Statistic Brain Research Institute (September 20, 2015). *Facebook Statistics*. http://www.statisticbrain.com/facebook-statistics/

loyalty (think hashtags and shareable content), and that means it's a must for influencers. As your influence grows, so will your followers and mentions, and this is what gets your brand exposure, engagement and traffic.

LinkedIn

You will need a business page and a personal profile on LinkedIn, because although this platform often gets overlooked, it is probably the best large social media platform designed perfectly for business and B2B marketing.

Many members are professionals connected to organizations and other influencers, so update LinkedIn often and make sure to be a part of 10 to 20 groups in your niche. It is a good idea to contribute to the groups at least once a week. LinkedIn users expect value-added contributions on the platform. And don't neglect Pulse; it is part of LinkedIn and is ideal for aspiring thought leaders.

Google+

Honestly, right now Google + is in total flux. While the site still exists and millions of people use it, it could be taken down tomorrow. Google could also potentially make a major push for it. But for now, I recommend using it sparingly.

YouTube

YouTube is incredibly powerful. It is the third most visited website on the planet and enjoys one billion unique viewers every month.[8] It is also the second largest search engine in existence, meaning that it has beaten both Bing and Yahoo out, solidifying Google's dominance.

Perhaps most important, YouTube reaches more adult viewers than any cable network.[9] You can create a video, set up an ad and

[8] Edward, Tony (July 24, 2015). "YouTube Ranking Factors: Getting Ranked In The Second Largest Search Engine." *Search Engine Land.* http://searchengineland.com/youtube-ranking-factors-getting-ranked-second-largest-search-engine-225533
[9] Ibid.

generate thousands of views for a few dollars – and if you don't, you'll be throwing away the chance to establish your authority for everyone using YouTube to search for your business, service or sphere of influence. I highly recommend you have a YouTube presence.

Pinterest

Only certain types of business owners will want to focus on Pinterest. Generally, the site is best for fashion, design, retail, food and beverage and related areas. I would recommend really looking to see if your demographic is present on Pinterest before putting in the time to make it work for you. Read this Pinterest guide for more information (https://ignitevisibility.com/the-definitive-guide-to-pinterest-marketing/).

Instagram

Instagram is fast becoming one of the most popular social media networks. It is extremely visual, but even if you don't create large amounts of high-end visual content, you can build a following by engaging with others on the platform. In this article, you can read everything you need to know about Instagram marketing (https://ignitevisibility.com/instagram-marketing/).

HARO

HARO stands for Help a Reporter Out. The website is a gold mine for editorial coverage. Simply sign up and you will get 3 emails a day that contain requests from reporters. These requests range from article interviews to TV spots. It is one of the fastest and easiest ways to get PR coverage for you and grow your influencer status.

Tumblr

Technically a platform for blogging, Tumblr hosts users' microblogs. Each microblog is filled with highly visual, shareable multimedia. This is a great place for viral content and memes, and it's easy to navigate via niche, making it a great place for ambitious influencers.

Reddit

Reddit is a cross between a news site and a social media platform. It's far more than the basic headlines or articles that are shared there because users virally share and vote up headlines. Popular Reddit users build loyal followings of news addicts (according to Pew, Reddit is the platform with the highest percentage of news readers[10]) who love to share and comment on information.

This makes it a potentially powerful marketing and influencing tool. To build influence, find your target communities in subreddits and engage with them by sharing and commenting on relevant, valuable headlines.

---

[10] Lunden, Ingrid (November 14, 2013). " Pew Social Media Study: 30% Of The U.S. Gets News Via Facebook; Reddit Has The Most News-Hungry Regular Users." *Techcrunch.* http://techcrunch.com/2013/11/14/pew-social-media-study-30-of-the-u-s-gets-news-via-facebook-reddit-has-the-most-news-hungry-regular-users/

Do not try to promote your products or services on Reddit. They will shut you down fast.

Yelp

Yelp provides user-generated ratings and reviews of businesses concerned with food, drink, shopping and entertainment. Researchers have found that Yelp is such a powerful tool for promoting unknown brands that it's eroding the brand strength of even the biggies like McDonald's.[11]

For the aspiring influencer, this is fantastic news; social media platforms like Yelp can allow you to narrow the gap and gain authority through your official brand profile page or as a reviewer. Using Yelp for your influencer strategy depends a great deal on who you are trying to influence and your business goals.

---

[11] Mourdoukoutas, Panos (July 22, 2014). "Are Yelp Stars Killing McDonald's Brand Advantage?" *Forbes Magazine*. http://www.forbes.com/sites/panosmourdoukoutas/2014/07/22/are-yelp-stars-killing-mcdonalds-brand-advantage/

Periscope and Meerkat

Periscope and Meerkat are two apps that are meant for live steaming online. Simply sign up, push a button, and you will immediately be presenting to the entire world from your phone.

Over 66% of American adults are consuming live streaming media, and it is one of the fastest growing digital mediums right now. Use these tools to build a following and become well-known in your space. For the record, Periscope is more than two times larger than Meerkat, as far as users.

Secondary Social Media Sites

In this section, we cover other social media sites you should know but do not necessarily need to be active on. Unless your demographic is there.

Flickr

This platform is first and foremost a photo-sharing site. This means you can best use it to build your influence by driving traffic to your other online pages, building your brand. Obviously, you need great images to succeed on Flickr, and you also need to make sure that anything you put on Flickr is strongly linked to your other platforms, profiles, e stores and sites.

Xing

Xing is a site designed like an international version of LinkedIn; it is a global platform for professional networking and recruitment. With over 8 million users from all over the world (albeit mostly in Europe), Xing features more than 34,000 niche groups that are home to business owners, organizations and influencers in many industries. It also hosts more than 150,000 live, online professional events each year and routinely adds new features. It's not as big as LinkedIn yet, but it is far more international and highly interactive.

RenRen

RenRen is the Facebook of China. It is particularly popular among millennial users, and users share content quickly and easily. It is worth your attention because experts say that over 91 percent of Chinese people use social media (compared to around 67 percent of Americans), and RenRen is home to about 54 million users every month – mostly young and connecting via mobile.[12] This means a huge segment of young people influencing trends are there, ready to connect and develop a relationship with your brand.

Disqus

Disqus is actually more of a social media management tool than a platform. It merits your attention because it can improve your user experience and help you protect your brand by filtering spam, tracking and analyzing comments and notifying you about comments to posts and other engagement metrics. Furthermore, its advanced features make upvoting and social monitoring,

---

[12] Simcott, Richard (February 26, 2014). "Social Media fast facts: China." *eModeration*. http://www.emoderation.com/social-media-fast-facts-china/

essential for influencers, possible.

Vine

This free site (more commonly used in app form) lets users record, view, share and comment on six-second video clips. Vine skews heavily toward memes and viral clips that are simple to share instantly, and you can often create your new Vine material in seconds.

Vine is a fantastic way to provide super-fast instructions and other useful content which helps you strengthen yourself as an authority, and it is being used by big brands to creatively entertain the 40 million Vine users who love to interact.[13] Let your creativity and knowledge shine in an entertaining way and you'll win over the Vine crowd easily and maintain their loyalty as you produce more.

---

[13] Fiegerman, Seth (August 20, 2013). "Vine Tops 40 Million Users." *Mashable*. http://mashable.com/2013/08/20/vine-40-million-registered-users/#PK99SYkzPuqo

WhatsApp

WhatsApp is an easy to use, almost free way to send and receive text-style messages to anyone on the platform. It is now the world's most popular messaging platform and was bought by Facebook for $19 billion. This is because real-time marketing and influencing is the wave of the future, especially for new ideas and products geared toward millennials.

Because the format is as intimate as sending someone a personal message, WhatsApp gives you the chance to really engage and build loyalty with users as you answer their questions in real time, sending them funny, attractive videos and images. Absolut Vodka[14] and Klik Chocolate[15] are among the big companies using WhatsApp to reach a new audience.

---

[14] Ferrao, Sheldon (November 17, 2013). "The First Whatsapp Marketing Campaign: Absolut Vodka Unique Access Party." *HashSlush*. http://www.hashslush.com/the-first-whatsapp-marketing-campaign-absolut-unique-access/

[15] More2Spot.com staff (2013). "Chocolate Vendor Goes Whatsapp." *More2Spot*. http://www.more2spot.com/en/sales-and-marketing-organisations/21-chocolate-vendor-goes-whats-app

Vk.com

Russians use social media more actively than anyone else worldwide, and all 100 million Russian social media users are on VK.[16] VK is similar to Facebook but has an extremely powerful search function that is much more sophisticated than Facebook's, pulling results from all over the web.

Huge brands like Samsung and Coca-Cola already use VK to reach niche communities and track the progress of their marketing with the VK analytics. Do not ignore the over 50 million very active daily users on this site.

Medium

Medium is a sort of hybrid platform that combines the best features of a blogging platform – a social media platform and an online magazine. You can use it to distill and promote your brand voice as an influencer by

---

[16] Morgan, Gareth (April 23, 2014). "What is VK? Your Guide to Russia's Largest Social Network." *MarketingTech*.
http://www.marketingtechnews.net/news/2014/apr/23/what-is-vk-your-guide-to-russias-largest-social-network/

publishing excellent content that the Medium algorithm rewards by promoting and curating.

I've written a few articles for Medium. Perhaps the best part is that they email the articles to all your Twitter followers. That helps with additional promotion. The creators of Medium were also part of the creation of Twitter and Blogger.

Meetup

Meetup allows you to connect with influential people in your niche or industry, either through existing groups or by starting your own.

When you frequently engage with the meetup, you gain connections and credibility in your area; you will also find opportunities to give talks and further increase your influence as a featured speaker. You also gain the motivational benefits of a mastermind group as you grow your influence. If you can start a successful meetup in your niche, you will be the go-to source in the community for on-point expertise.

Snapchat

Snapchat lets you send users a temporary picture message that can also include text and art. Especially useful for B2C businesses targeting teens, experts think Snapchat has more than 30 million active users and fields more than 400 million messages every day.[17]

Snapchat promotes more community interaction based on speed, and since updates disappear quickly, users check the platform frequently. If your influencer plans include a younger audience that values technology, Snapchat can be a great choice for fostering personal interaction and developing your brand without the competition present on other platforms.

Yahoo Answers

---

[17] Kyriacou, Chris (April 25, 2015). "5 Reasons Why Brands Should Be Using Snapchat." *Social Media Today*. http://www.socialmediatoday.com/social-networks/2015-04-25/5-reasons-why-brands-should-be-using-snapchat

Technically not a social media platform, Yahoo Answers is, nevertheless, a place to build authority as an expert and engage with others, driving traffic elsewhere. Answers provided here are searchable, too, so phrase things with SEO in mind without being over the top.

Use this platform to answer questions in an informed way and provide links for further information at the end of your answers. But be careful not to spam Yahoo answers too much. I admit at one point I was asking questions just so I could direct people off the site and on to a site I was promoting. Do this too much and you will get banned.

Quora

Quora is like the better-educated, more-reputable cousin of Yahoo Answers; people go to the Quora Q&A community to ask questions that only experts can answer. Like Yahoo Answers, search engines crawl Quora. Users are smart and have great credentials overall, and the platform verifies user profiles, so Quora answers are authoritative.

Quora is vastly underutilized and enjoys more than 1.5 million visitors worldwide every month.[18] Use Quora to establish your voice as an expert and build trust and a following by organically contributing to conversations without being salesy; only comment when you can truly add value to the discussion. Bonus: get great new ideas for content based on what people are asking about in your niche and connect with other influencers.

MySpace

This may come as a surprise, but MySpace still gets more than 50 million users every month![19] Most of the users on MySpace are young, ages 17 to 25, and interested in social activities and taking in pop culture.

---

[18] Kandler, Jessica (July 9, 2015). "10 Reasons Why Marketers Should Use Quora." *Semrush*. https://www.semrush.com/blog/10-reasons-why-marketers-should-use-quora/

[19] Shields, Mike (January 14, 2015). "MySpace Still Reaches 50 Million People Each Month." *Wall Street Journal Blogs*. http://blogs.wsj.com/cmo/2015/01/14/myspace-still-reaches-50-million-people-each-month/

If your target audience is hip and young enough to think MySpace is ironic, this is a platform you should consider. It's also one of the best platforms for the music industry, so you'll want to spend time here if you work in this field.

Ryze

Ryze is sort of a cross between Facebook and LinkedIn with the added twist of being geared toward entrepreneurs in particular. Your profile or home page on Ryze is designed for networking, and with more than 1,000 organizations and 500,000 members in over 200 countries around the world using the platform, there is plenty of opportunity there.

Use this network to share authoritative information in relevant groups, as you would on LinkedIn, to build your authority, and meet other influencers. This site is still fairly small, but it has that grass roots feel to it and some very active members.

Affluence

Affluence is the Facebook for the rich, with a user requirement of a minimum net worth of $1 million or annual salary of $200K. The emphasis here is on not only elite culture and wealth, but also philanthropy. Interestingly, you can also join even if you don't meet the financial requirements if five existing members invite you.

Affluence users share information on pet charities and network; they also enjoy various perks like access to events, a user marketplace and a 24-hour concierge service. If you can use this platform you should because you will be interacting with some of the world's most important investors and influencers.

Foursquare

Foursquare originated as an app to "check in" from place to place on other social media platforms, but today is making use of the rich check in data it accumulated for years to provide deep local search capabilities.

Foursquare covers 60 million locations, and like Yelp, its users rank and review the places they've visited. The new version of Foursquare allows you to build expertise and gain "mayorship" by sharing useful information about local businesses.

Biznik

Biznik is a platform for networking and the exchange of ideas between independent business owners. Whereas LinkedIn is very focused on offering and applying for jobs, Biknik is for entrepreneurs and business owners to engage in B2B networking.

As you share your knowledge about business ownership, offer free trainings and meet people in your industry, you establish your authority and meet other influencers. Biznik is far more focused than larger platforms so it also presents less noise and more value. Biznik offers added SEO benefits as it is considered to be an authoritative site.

Cmypitch.com

Cmypitch.com offers a balance of social and business networking between entrepreneurs and investors. The site lets you upload your own video pitch to investors free of charge and access high-quality "how to" guides from higher profile influencers. If you have this kind of entrepreneurial guidance to offer, this is a great place to establish and grow your authority.

Cofoundr

Cofoundr is designed to help businesses, designers, programmers, entrepreneurs and investors network with the goal of creating new ventures as well as share knowledge and advice. It is filled with influencers and experts that you can learn from, network with and engage with to build your own influence.

EFactor

EFactor is very similar to Cmypitch and

Cofoundr. This business social networking platform links investors and entrepreneurs from around the world for ventures and for sharing information and strategies. This is another good place to establish yourself as an expert in your field.

Entrepreneur Connect

Entrepreneur Connect is another social networking site designed for businesses. The focus here, however, is less on winning investment money and more on sharing information and self-help. This is a good place to work to establish yourself as an authority as the information is considered more reputable since active self-promotion is frowned upon. Just be sure that your information is truly useful and worthy of influencer status.

Fast Pitch

Fast Pitch is one of the best-known business networking sites, and its focus is on efficiency, ROI and cutting out the fluff. The site also offers tools like blog promotion, e-mail marketing, direct mail marketing, and press distribution for users. Clearly, in this setting, you have to have true expertise and authority to engage with others, so this is another strong location for influencers.

StumbleUpon

StumbleUpon is essentially a specialized search engine for interesting and relevant content. For your content to thrive on StumbleUpon, it has to be high-quality; that's how it earns thumbs up and subsequently appears in the personalized feed of users. This is a great tool for influencers because it can help your advice, "how-tos," articles, infographics and other content to be seen by anyone interested in your area of influence.

Be Smart with Your Time, Select Sites that Matter

One of the most important parts of being a successful influencer is good time management. I do not want you to waste your time on all of these sites. I do want you to pick two to four and really own them.

Keep in mind, time is the most valuable thing we all have in life. You have to use it wisely. You could spend years developing a major following on StumbleUpon, but that would be a waste of time unless your demographic is there resulting in your influencing the people who are going to help you accomplish your business, personal and life goals.

> **Action Item**: Analyze your main influencers and competitors. Find out the social media sites they are spending the most time on. Review the list above and determine the best places for you to be spending your time on social media. Take that list and allocate a certain amount of time to each site per week. For example, Facebook one hour, Twitter one hour, YouTube two hours, etc. This will help you develop a personal plan. Put your focus in two to four social media sites.

Chapter 3: Getting Advanced, Getting Innovative, Getting Seen

So far, we've learned how influencers use blogging and guest posting to develop a following. We reviewed the basics of SEO and the importance of knowing your audience. We learned how to educate others while befriending and leveraging other influencers. We identified the most important social media sites to participate in and the importance of using your time wisely. Now, it's time to identify the tools you can use to make that job easier.

Smart Tools to Give You the Edge Most People Fail to Find

Influencers have expertise, but they also know how to make the most of tools to save labor, time and money. This is my list of the best tools for influencers and how you can use them to enhance your authority.

Now, there are a lot of tools listed in this section. It is important that you know all of them, but if you are not ready to learn about every single one, you can always come back to this section later.

BuzzSumo

BuzzSumo helps you analyze types of content to see which subjects garner the most attention. This, in turn, lets you find the key influencers working in your content area so you can reach out to them.

BuzzSumo also lets you see what your competitors are doing with content on certain subjects and what keywords they are using. Finally, this tool helps you decide which social media platforms are working best for your topic areas. It can even show you which users have shared content similar to yours in the past; you can target the same people as you share your content and join the influencer conversation.

SumoMe

SumoMe is really a set of tools to use on your WordPress website or blog – some are free; some are pay tools. Among the tools are heat maps that show you your website's strengths and weaknesses, and list builder and share tools to help grow your circle of influence.

Since part of influencing is having an ever-growing list of followers who will use and share your work, building up that list is critical. SumoMe works well at growing these lists, so this is the principal benefit of using it.

FollowerWonk

FollowerWonk is a tool designed to help you gain followers on Twitter, specifically. It can allow you to search bios of Twitter accounts based on keywords, interests, location and other factors so you can find people who will be likely to share your content – and whose sharing will be fruitful for you based on their own follower stats. It can also help you analyze and compare the demographics of your followers and those of competitors or influencers you hope to emulate.

Klout

Often debated and sometimes feared, Klout is a platform specifically designed for influencers. Its purpose is to assess how much influence each user has based on an algorithm that analyzes your content, engagement and overall impact on various social media platforms.

Think of Klout as a tool with a specific, useful metric for your own benefit, not anyone else's; you can see how you rank and then set specific goals to work up to a higher score and level of influence. The more content you produce that is high-quality and engages others, the higher your Klout score will climb.

SEMrush

SEMrush lets you see both how well your own website is doing and how well the sites of your competitors are doing. You can use it to see how much paid and unpaid traffic you're getting, how well you're doing with your target keywords and how you're ranked against others – and you can see the same information for other sites.

When you see someone in your niche that's head and shoulders above everyone else, you want to know how they're doing it so you can improve your own performance. SEMrush lets you do that. Naturally, as you see who these heavy hitters are in your niche, you find influencers to reach out to and perhaps partner with.

SpyFu

SpyFu is great at helping you suss out the marketing formula of competitors, and this means it can also help you identify influencers and borrow their best strategies. It also helps you build up more authority for your website by boosting organic traffic. Finally, it offers AdWords tips which any influencer can and will use.

Screaming Frog

Screaming Frog is a very popular SEO tool and overall time saver. It helps you find everything from broken links and Google Analytics code, to redirects and duplicate content. You can use it on any website – yours or those of competitors and other influencers – almost instantly. You can use this tool to crawl competitors' sites and find out what they are doing to rank well. You can also use the tool to make sure your website is structurally sound.

Majestic

Majestic is one of the best tools in the industry for checking links to a website. You can use this tool to see who is linking to you or to your competitors. One of the main ways people use it is to review competitor links and then use that list as a road map to build their own links.

Moz Open Site Explorer

Like Majestic, Moz tools all allow you to see the "domain authority" of any given site – yours or someone else's. This is a metric created by Moz which uses more than 40 signals to predict how well pages will rank in searches. Use OSE specifically to find the best link building and content opportunities, track your websites authority individually and against competitors over time, and to engage in focused, effective link building.

Fresh Web Explorer

Fresh Web Explorer from Moz lets you research and compare links and mentions with your top competitors. You can set up an alert so you can see anytime someone mentions or links to your two biggest competitors – but not you.

It also allows you to compare based on keywords; it searches millions of URLs and RSS feeds to get your results. As an influencer, you want to find places where you're not getting into the conversation naturally so you can build a presence there and fix the weakness.

Vocus/Cision

In 2014, Vocus and Cision combined forces; the company continues to offer its social and PR software. It's useful for influencers because it provides so much − analytics; blog, news and social media monitoring; a media database with more than 400,000 bloggers, journalists and writers; and a platform for email campaigns and press release distribution.

Just like when you use HARO, you can monitor queries using Vocus/Cision; however, this tool also allows you to distribute your own work independent of queries. It also provides metrics on ad value, impressions, and whether your mentions are neutral or positive so you can respond to mentions of you, your brand and your work for further engagement.

Google Analytics

Every website needs Google Analytics. With Google Analytics, you can assess your social media ROI and influence using the conversions report. You can also see which platforms are strongest for you. Overall, Google Analytics is still the most detailed source of metrics out there, and it is free. There is a paid version, Google Analytics Premium, but you only need it if you have millions of visitors a month.

Google Content Experiments

Google Content Experiments is of the easiest ways to split test one page vs. another online. You can use this tool to see which version of a web page performs better and has a higher conversion rate.

Google Search Console

Formerly Google Webmaster Tools, Google Search Console helps you repair issues on your site. In addition, it allows you to manipulate the way your site is indexed in Google and gives you specific analytics metrics. This is a must-have free tool that all websites should install.

Amazon (create an eBook)

Creating an eBook is easy on Amazon, and it's a fantastic way to prove just how much value your expertise can add to your niche area. eBooks are useful to your followers and potential followers, cheap to produce, and can boost your authority. The only caveat here is that your content must be absolutely top quality; don't waste this opportunity on anything less than your best work.

HelloBar

HelloBar lets you easily display messages at the top of your WordPress website. You can use your message for a variety of purposes including collecting email addresses, directing users to your landing page, or just making an announcement or disseminating a message. It's easy to use and effective; why would you give up the chance to get more information from your visitors?

Topsy

Topsy is a search tool that you can use to monitor mentions of you and your brand in real time. It offers both analytical information and sentiment metrics and is especially useful for Twitter users since it operates in real time and sifts through large amounts of information quickly.

One potential drawback is that it focuses not on all mentions, but instead, on the most popular or influential mentions; however, you could see this as a benefit since this means it inherently directs you to the most influential conversations to join in and to the top influencers in your area.

SocialMention.com

SocialMention.com is a great tool for seeing interactions and mentions of you and your brand. You can limit the results based on source or timeframe, and see top hashtags, keywords, sources and users as well. Most critically for influencers, socialmention.com lets you assess passion (how likely the mention is to be repeated), reach (the actual influence measure), sentiment (negative, neutral or positive), and brand strength (how often you're being discussed).

CrazyEgg

CrazyEgg is a powerful heat map tool that you install into your page as a script. It tracks how site visitors engage with your content, how many people scrolled to various sections on a given page (in other words, how well you're keeping them and which areas need more work to retain visitors), and which portions of the page get the most traffic so you can place your best content there and improve the overall user experience your site offers.

Unbounce

This tool for building landing pages lets you drag and drop widgets and edit easily. The result is that you can easily add an opt-in form and signup. Unbounce also lets you split test your landing pages to get the best results. Since opt-in rates are a concrete sign of more influence, use this tool to make sure you get as many opt-ins as you can.

Optin Monster

This tool lets you create simple, appealing pop-ups for your website. Popups are very effective at building up your email sign-up rate, which is key to your growth as an influencer. The tool can also be limited to appear only when certain places on the site are clicked on.

WooBox

This is a great tool for creating contests, coupons, giveaways, polls and sweepstakes on Facebook – in other words, a tool for building meaningful engagement and brand loyalty on the biggest social media platform today. It also lets you manage all of these ventures from one place and see stats for each engagement event.

Hootsuite

Hootsuite is a great tool for monitoring chatter and mentions of you and your brand across most of the major social media platforms like Facebook, LinkedIn and Twitter (more than 35 platforms are available).

You can add a multitude of "streams" to your dashboard, each based on a different keyword or phrase; and then, you just sit back and watch your mentions in real time. This is a great way to be able to engage with people on topics that are important to you without jumping from platform to platform. It also lets you schedule your social media posts to maximize results.

Twitter Feed

This tool from Twitter lets you place a feed on your website or blog, and feed your blog to Facebook, LinkedIn, Twitter and other platforms. You can watch your stats in real time to see what works and why; this lets you modify your strategies as needed.

Optimizely

This is one of the top split testing and conversion rate optimization tools in the world. This is a tool that can help even small businesses personalize their marketing approach. It does this by providing data and analytics for your visitors so you can target based on behavior in real time.

This is a powerful tool for influencers, especially given its Recommended Audiences tool. Recommended Audiences assesses your greatest chances for personalization and then uses predictive analytics to identify groups that will be meaningful to your work; this way you can focus and prioritize your outreach and engagement efforts efficiently.

Google Alerts

This is an easy and free way to get updated on mentions of any keyword online. Take advantage and set up a Google Alert now. Found here (https://www.google.com/alerts), it is a good idea to set up an alert for your company name and your own name.

More about Tools

If you want to read more about tools, I recommend checking out these posts:

The Big List: 80 Of The Hottest SEO, Social Media & Digital Analytics Tools For Marketers: http://marketingland.com/80-hottest-seo-social-media-digital-analytics-tools-marketers-112446

Social Brand Mentions: Key Tools To Find And Fully Capitalize On Them For Marketing: http://marketingland.com/social-brand-mentions-find-fully-capitalize-marketing-139876

- **Action Item: Use tools to respond and capitalize on mentions.** Now, if you see that someone has mentioned you using a tool like Google Alerts, SocialMention.com or Fresh Web Explorer, what do you do? Well, if someone is praising you, take advantage.

I generally like to use this kind of mention as an opportunity to establish a new relationship. Whether you ask for a link to the website, propose a guest blog or discuss setting up a joint webinar, you need to take advantage of mentions.

Try an email like this. Edit to make it your own, and express only ideas that you mean:

Hi <name>,

I saw that you mentioned us in <insert URL here>. I really appreciate the mention, and I am a big fan of <where it was mentioned>.

I am going to share your post on our social media outlets. We have <x number> Twitter followers and <x number Facebook fans>.

Would you please link our name to our website? Also, can I write a guest blog for your site?

Here are a few ideas:

<Idea One>
<Idea Two>

I would also love it if you would write a guest blog for us or if I could interview you for our website.

I am looking forward to speaking with you and thank you again!

Sincerely,

Keep a Google doc of everyone you interact with. I am so happy that I have done this over the years. I have a list of places I guest post. After I write a blog, I can go down the list and select the best option. Of course, that site will always have to approve it, but at this point, I generally know who will accept what.

Why You Will Lose Without Social Media Ads and Where to Run Them

Now, I want to talk about growing your social media communities with ads. If you do not run ads, you are wasting so much time. Why spend five years trying to get 1,000 likes on Facebook when you can spend $500 and get them in one day? Trust me on this one. If you do this, you can have thousands of Twitter followers, Facebook fans, etc., in a week. Social media ads are cheap, and they work.

Choosing the Social Media Site

Before you start running ads, you need to make sure you are using the right social media website. For example, LinkedIn is an excellent site for an internet marketing company to drive leads, but it would be a poor choice for a retail brand looking to reach customers.

Instead, Pinterest would be a much better option for retail. Make sure to take the time to do your research and find the most effective communities for your product or service. For more on this, you can read this post: Where to Spend Time on Social Media for Business (https://ignitevisibility.com/where-to-spend-time-on-social-media-for-business/).

Take the Time to Establish a Solid Foundation

Now that you have selected the network, make sure to take the time to establish a solid social media profile foundation. Regardless of the website, lay the groundwork by doing 10 to 15 posts, adding a profile image and banners, filling out all the information the sites request and making sure you have a complete and professional profile. This will ensure that when people visit your page after clicking on a social media ad, they convert.

Focus Your Demographic

If you are not careful about how you select your demographic when you set up these ads, you won't see the results you want. You might grow your community quickly, but the only thing it will be good for is bragging about how many people are in it.

For example, on Facebook, you can setup an ad to gain likes from specific countries, like Malaysia, for about one penny per like. Many people do this so they can make it look like their page has tens of thousands (to hundreds of thousands) of followers. However, almost none of them are relevant for your ultimate purpose.

Generally, it's best to really hone-in on location, age, interest, keywords and other criteria. This will result in your posts generating better engagement and direct business. I really recommend that when you set up your ads, you take the time to establish a highly targeted demographic.

Run Your Ads

Now that the preliminaries have been taken care of, let's talk about the basics of running community growth ads. Many websites with social components offer advertising options, but here we will focus on the most popular options: Pinterest, Instagram, Facebook, LinkedIn, Twitter and YouTube.

Promote Your Content with Pinterest Promoted Pins

If you have a U.S.-based business, you can promote your pins on Pinterest.[20] Promoted Pins allow you to advertise to people who are in your target market but don't follow you. The idea is that they'll engage and begin following your boards and business profile. In addition, you may sell a product or service.

Advertise on Instagram to Boost Engagement

Instagram offers numerous ad formats and solutions[21], and it is open to all businesses. You can purchase the ads through Facebook's self-serve platform and through Instagram's Ads API. Facebook and Instagram together compose the world's largest mobile ad network, offering unparalleled distribution. While the new Instagram ads focus on website clicks, app installs or video views, you can use each of these targeting types to get more visibility for your content. If done right, this will result in more followers.

---

[20] Read here for more details on how this works: https://business.pinterest.com/en/promoted-pins?utm_medium=2023&utm_source=31&utm_campaign=GAdspp
[21] https://business.instagram.com/advertising/

Grow "Likes" Quickly on Facebook with "Page Like Ads"

Facebook is a social media platform which is a "go to" option for many digital marketers. That's because the company provides highly targeted ad capabilities based on interests, demographics and more.[22]

But if you are going to be on Facebook for business-related social marketing, you need a community. With Facebook Page Like Ads, you can get a new page "like" for a cost ranging from a few cents to a few dollars, quickly growing your community. If you don't have at least a few thousand page likes, or tens of thousands if you are a major brand, I recommend you make an investment and run these ads.

Promote Your Page Content with LinkedIn

---

[22] https://www.facebook.com/business/ads-guide/page-likes/?toggle0=Photo

LinkedIn allows you to run targeted audience ads or sponsored content ads.[23] Both are highly effective for different goals. For community growth, try running sponsored content ads around your page updates. If you have a new product, big company news, or a piece of content you want to get noticed, this is the place to get your content seen by other business owners. By promoting content over time, you will get more people to "follow" your business page and know your brand.

Get More Twitter Followers

Twitter offers a variety of advertising options to grow your community.[24] Out of all the options available, the best way to grow a community with Twitter ads is through a Promoted Accounts ad. If you are a business looking to get more Twitter followers and better distribution for your content, you can expand your community for around fifty

---

[23] https://www.linkedin.com/ad/start
[24] https://business.twitter.com/solutions/grow-followers?lang=en&location=na

cents to a few dollars per new follower.[25]

Tweet engagement ads are also good, but they do not result in as many direct followers.[26] Instead, they simply bring more visibility to a Tweet.

Boost YouTube Channel Views and Subscribers

As the largest video site in the world, YouTube has advertising options that can get you thousands of video views at a very inexpensive rate. On average, a view costs between 10 to 30 cents. You can run video ads on YouTube to get your content noticed and attract subscribers.[27]

When setting up your YouTube ads, you can choose to advertise the video view page or the main channel page. Based on my experience, if you advertise the main channel

---

[25] https://business.twitter.com/solutions/promoted-accounts?lang=en&location=na

[26] https://business.twitter.com/solutions/tweet-engagements

[27] https://www.youtube.com/yt/advertise/

page, you will get more subscribers. If you advertise the video page, you will get more views.

Spending a few hundred to a few thousand dollars on social media community growth and content promotion can make all the difference for your social media marketing. I highly recommend that you take the time to find the right network for your business and then make an investment in community growth. Without a large and targeted community, you are not an influencer.

- **Action Item**: Determine a social media advertising budget that you are comfortable with. Next, allocate that budget based on the sites you want to focus on most. Use that money to grow your social media communities and promote your content.

Using the New Wave of Native Advertising to Get Content over Ten Times the Reach

Just like you should run ads to grow a community, you should also run ads around your content and promotions to get them more exposure. If you know how to use native advertising, you will be a better influencer.

Native advertising is essentially a paid advertisement that functions a little bit differently than a traditional paid advertisement. Using written content, native advertising is essentially an ad that's disguised as original content by the platform. Though they clearly say "ad," they're still interspersed with other "non-ads" in the results.

Advertisers have found that these ads are extremely profitable. Plenty of people continue to click on those ads, and buy those products.

Native advertising takes the same principles as these other ads and inserts them into written content.

In a magazine for example, native advertising might appear as an insertion that's written as another article in the magazine, but is actually an advertisement. It's designed to fit seamlessly into the content that surrounds it, which is why it's often mistaken for actual content.

The reason native advertising is so effective is that these "camouflaged" ads are usually better received by their target audiences. Because they don't "feel" like advertisements, people are more inclined to view them and consume their content.

In traditional advertising, a graphic advertisement can be easily ignored, as people are constantly inundated with marketing ads throughout their day. Native advertising allows brands and influencers to get their message across with a greater likelihood that it gets consumed by the target audience.

Support Content Marketing with Native Advertising

If you want to be an influencer, you need to embrace content marketing and native advertising as the means for getting a marketing message across. You need to market yourself and your content just the way a marketing manager would market a brand.

Content marketing is not advertising, while native advertising very much is. However, one important distinction is that native advertising can greatly support your content marketing:

- Viewers spend nearly the same amount of time reading editorial content and native ads – 2 seconds and 1 second, respectively.
- 70% of individuals want to learn about products through content rather than through traditional advertising.
- People view native ads 53% more than banner ads.

What you are paying for with native ads is the ability to "rent" the platform to increase your distribution.

After the content is created and approved, it's tagged with a "warning" of sorts that may say something like "Advertisement" or "Paid Advertisement." This creates some transparency within the platform because it doesn't completely disrupt the experience as say, a television commercial advertisement might.

Recently, Alan Bush (Ignite Visibility's Director of Strategy) and I did a webinar on the most important SEO initiatives for 2016. I ran native ads on YouTube and Facebook. Without these ads, the post might have had tens of likes on Facebook and hundreds on YouTube videos. But by spending $300 on native ads, I was able to get over 7,000 YouTube views and 600 Facebook likes in just a few days.

Action Item: Use native advertising to promote your content, your webinars, and your videos. Anything you want to get exposure for! Keep in mind, if you spend $50 on a native ad only get limited results, you can always up your budget and run the ad again. A very common strategy to run native ads over and over again until a piece of content reaches the target number of people.

How You Can Use Viral Marketing Concepts for Exponential Reach

If you can make something go viral, you really win as an influencer. It will build your following and do a great deal to jump start your status. Let's take a moment to discuss what it takes to make a piece of content go viral.

Know What It Takes to Go Viral

First, it is important to point something out. There is content that *actually* goes viral, and then there is content that only *appears* to go viral. The first is content that, through a series of person to person recommendations, has resulted in hundreds of thousands to millions of views. The second is a piece of content that has simply had significant ad dollars thrown behind it.

Any piece of content can appear to have gone viral simply because the company behind the content had a large advertising plan and a great promotional strategy (or they may have paid for fake traffic or shares).

Shock Value Is Important

The type of content that goes viral generally has shock value on some level. Essentially, it catches the person engaging it by surprise. This shock triggers a feeling in this person that the content is unique and interesting, prompting the emotional response of quickly passing it on.

Evoking a sense of shock in the audience is one of the best strategies for developing viral content (or marketing content in general). While this is the case, it is important to understand that there are many ways to create this shock; shock may come about through humor, fear, romance, etc.

Below, we see three of the most shared posts on Twitter on the subject of content marketing:

- 10 Content Marketing Mistakes that the Amateurs Make
  Shock: Person reads this and does not want to make an amateur mistake

- Content Marketing, The Definitive Truth About It
  Shock: Person reads this and needs to know the truth

- 16 Killer Content Marketing Resources All Entrepreneurs Need
  Shock: Person does not want to miss out on needed resources

The Formula for Viral Marketing

So, is there a secret formula for making something go viral? The content must evoke an emotional response in the audience at the right level. Also, the larger the promotion of the content the better the chance that it will go viral; in other words, the more people who see the content the more likely it is to evoke an emotional response in someone and get shared.

You can create a basic model for this. If you show the content to 100 people and 10 share it, you have a virality level of 10%. You can then plug this in and create your formula:

(Virality Level) x (Number of People Who See the Content) = Number of Shares

The formula repeats itself as the content is shared over time and more as more people are subjected to the content. Generally, each viral post has a life cycle that depends on promotion and virality level.

Indications Something Might Go Viral

For any given business, there are an average number of shares a post will get. This is generally based on the quality of the content. For example, our Ignite Visibility University posts usually get between 50 and 200 shares per post.

This is really important because it allows us to define viral. Viral means different things to different businesses and websites. We might consider one of our posts to have gone viral if it gets 1,500 shares, because it is a large number outside of our normal distribution. On the other hand, when I post an article on Search Engine Land or Entrepreneur, those posts almost always get between 1,000 and 3,000 shares.

Essentially, going viral means achieving 10 or 20 times the normal numbers.

How a Large Community Influences Viral Marketing

The number of followers is important, but the number of followers that are highly engaged is far more critical. Think about all the lovestruck girls that would interact with a

Justin Bieber post; he has very highly-engaged fans that interact with his posts.

On the other hand, think of a guy who bought 100,000 Twitter followers on Fiverr or one of the hundreds of "Twitter-followers-for-sale" websites out there; he won't get much (if anything) useful from that group.

How to Increase Your Chances of Going Viral

You need to have some level of understanding of what it takes for something to go viral if you want to become an influencer. This will help everything you do get more exposure.

We already know this is the equation:

(Virality Level) x (Number of People Who See the Content) = Number of Shares

So, how do you increase each element?

Boost your virality level:

- Have a great title
- Hit a pain point
- Make it emotional
- Answer a hard question
- Make it visually striking

Increase the number of people who see the content:

- Build a large social media community
- Run social media community building ads
- Run promoted posts as on social media
- Promote your content everywhere

Other best practices for going viral:

- Use persuasive language

These five words in the English language have been proven to be the most persuasive for conversions[28]:

[28] Ciotti, Gregory. "The 5 Most Persuasive Words in the English Language." *Copyblogger*. http://www.copyblogger.com/persuasive-copywriting-words/

- **Free.** This word has the potential to generate more conversions by as much as 73 percent because everyone loves free stuff.[29]
- **You.** Saying "you" has been shown to be almost as effective as calling someone by name in generating a response according to a study. Use "you" it is very powerful.
- **Because.** Holds the ability to produce 94 percent higher results because it encourages a person's willingness to take action.[30]
- **Instantly.** MRI studies have shown that our midbrain envisions instant gratification and prompts us to act, whereas our frontal cortex is engaged when we delay gratification.[31] The bottom line: for fast, almost automatic conversions, you want the midbrain to feel that instant gratification buzz.

---

[29] Ibid.; see the research of Dan Ariely for more on this: http://web.mit.edu/ariely/www/MIT/papers.shtml

[30] This is drawn from a classic experiment conducted by Robert Cialdini; he discusses it in his book *Influence: The Power of Persuasion*.

[31] See for example this study: http://www.emeraldinsight.com/doi/abs/10.1108/07363760710834807

- **New.** For a variety of reasons, the brain's reward center is activated when it sees "new," especially in conjunction with brands (and influencers) that are already trusted.[32]

Now these are great words, but it is more important what the words imply. You can use other words with similar meanings and get similar effects.

Best Words for More Shareable Content

When specific words are used, they increase the shareability of content on social media sites. This is especially true when they are grouped together or teamed up with other powerful words:

- **Secret.** This powerful word lets customers feel as though they are revealing a great mystery.

---

[32] Ciotti, Gregory. "The 5 Most Persuasive Words in the English Language." *Copyblogger.* http://www.copyblogger.com/persuasive-copywriting-words/

- **Increase.** Leads to more conversions by prompting readers to fulfill their desire for bigger and better.
- **Discover.** Causes readers to believe they are finding something new and unknown that holds amazing benefits.
- **Create.** Inspires readers to do more and encourages them to share their new creative discovery with others.
- **Promote.** Proven to trigger an actionable response, especially on social media.

The same goes for these words; you can use similar words and get similar results.

Powerful Call-to-Action Words and Phrases

A great call-to-action involves the fear of missing out. Certain words convince readers that something is scarce or in limited supply to drive action. Examples would be the following:

- **Limited offer.** Drives home the point that an offer may not be available if they wait to take advantage of a great deal.
- **Today only.** Readers love bargains and will jump on the opportunity.
- **Now.** Perfect for email subject lines, headlines and calls-to-action to produce instant conversions.
- **Hurry.** Implies the importance of haste to take advantage of a great offer. Combine with other actionable words to harness more power.
- **Exclusive.** Makes readers feel as though they are benefiting from a special deal with limited access.

Earning Trust and Gaining Influence with Words

There are certain words that are known to cause a reader to lose trust, especially adverbs and adjectives. Noted as the worst elements of speech for loss of trust, it's best to avoid them. In addition, the fewer words you use, the more trust you'll gain.

Action Item: Create 5 article titles using the words, or words similar to, the words listed above. Practice creating compelling titles that have the ability to go viral.

Chapter 4: Your Personal Plan of Action

In this chapter, you will be creating your plan of action for becoming an influencer. Creating a detailed plan with a timeline will help ensure that you achieve your influencer status. Do not skip this step.

The Most Important Part: Creating Your Influencer Plan of Action

Okay, so far in this book we have covered the following:

- Critical Components to Becoming a Real Influencer
- Three Types of Influencers – Who Will You Be?
- The Science and Psychology of Influence
- How You Can Use Targeted Content to Grow Your Influence
- How to Gain Influence Through Blogging

- Secrets to Guest Posting Like a Pro
- How You Can Use SEO to Drive Your Authority
- Be Innovative, Have Something to Say and Be Listened To
- Why and How You Need to Educate Others
- How to Befriend Influencers and Leverage Each Other
- Social Media Sites You Should Be Looking At
- Be Smart with Your Time, Select Sites that Matter
- Smart Tools to Give You the Edge Most People Fail to Find
- Why You Will Lose Without Social Media Ads and Where to Run Them
- Using the New Wave of Native Advertising to Get Content over Ten Times the Reach
- How You Can Use Viral Marketing Concepts for Exponential Reach

Now, it is time to turn this information into a specific plan so that you can become an influencer yourself.

Influencer Self Evaluation: Must Ask Questions

Answer each of these questions for yourself:

- What are your business goals, personal goals and life goals over the next 5, 10 and 20 years?

- What specifically do you need to achieve to get there?

- Who do you need to influence to reach those goals?

- Who are the people you want to influence? Which demographic works best for you?

- What are the top media outlets your demographic interacts with?

- What are the top social media sites your demographic interacts with?

- Who is the most well-known person in your industry? What self-promotion activities does that person use? How can you mimic what that person has done while also staying true to yourself and adding your own unique greatness to the mix?

- Who are the top influencers in your industry? What do these people do to promote themselves?

- Who are the mid-level influencers in your industry?

- What are the top events your demographic attends?

- What does your demographic like to do for fun?

- What are your industry hot buttons?

The Timeline: Review, Absorb, Customize, Become

To maximize your chances of success, follow a detailed plan with a timeline. Audit your progress periodically to ensure your strategies are working. Depending on your financial situation, do these tasks yourself or consider hiring an assistant or agency to help you. Here is an example plan that is very similar to the plan I use for myself and for my clients.

Month 1

- Determine your goals
- Determine who you want to influence
- Create your personal influencer guidelines
- Develop a blog
- Create your social media profiles
- Start your email list
- Respond to Help a Reporter Out three times a week
- Start to build a list of media contacts at three publications

Month 2

- Create an editorial calendar
- Blog two to four times a week
- Start sending out a bi-weekly email with your content
- Update social media profiles daily
- Interview other people for your blog post
- Mention other people in your blog and let them know via email or social media
- Start establishing guest blog connections
- Respond to Help a Reporter Out three times a week
- Add three more contacts to your list of media publications and begin pitching stories

Month 3

- Blog two to four times a week
- Update social media profiles daily
- Send out bi-weekly email
- Interview other people for your blog post
- Mention other people in your blog and let them know via email or social media
- Start guest blogging one to two times a month

- Start social media advertising for community growth
- Plan for your first webinar
- Respond to Help a Reporter Out three times a week
- Add three more contacts to your list of media publications and continue pitching two stories a month

Month 4

- Blog two to four times a week
- Update social media profiles daily
- Send out bi-weekly email
- Interview other people for your blog post
- Mention other people in your blog and let them know via email or social media
- Guest blog two times a month
- Continue social media advertising for community growth
- Speak at your first event
- Start planning your video marketing strategy
- Respond to Help a Reporter Out three times a week

- Add three more contacts to your list of media publications and continue pitching two stories a month

Month 5

- Blog two to four times a week
- Update social media profiles daily
- Send out bi-weekly email
- Interview other people for your blog post
- Mention other people in your blog and let them know via email or social media
- Guest blog two times a month
- Continue social media advertising for community growth
- Plan next speaking event and webinar
- Launch first video
- Respond to Help a Reporter Out three times a week
- Add three more contacts to your list of media publications and continue pitching two stories a month

Ongoing

- Continue blogging weekly

- Continue updating social media profiles daily
- Send out bi-weekly emails
- Interview other people for your blog post
- Mention other people in your blog and let them know via email or social media
- Guest blog two times a month
- Continue social media advertising for community growth
- Either speak at an event or do a webinar each month
- Launch a new video each month
- Send out press releases at least four times a year
- Create infographics, interactive content and industry studies
- Respond to Help a Reporter Out three times a week

Measuring Your Success

Generally, you will know if you are doing well if:

- Your traffic in Google Analytics is going up

- People are mentioning you on your choice social media sites and those mentions are increasing
- You are getting closer to your goals
- More opportunities are coming in and things are increasing exponentially
- You are generating business in your field

Final Takeaways

I want you to become an influencer in your industry. If you have any questions about the content in this book, you can Tweet a question to me here @johnelincoln. If you follow the plan in this book, you will reach influencer status. It is a proven method.

Now, you just need to get out there and do it. Who will you be in life? Will you be a follower? Or will you be an influencer?

44665174R00100

Made in the USA
San Bernardino, CA
21 January 2017